The Waytravelers
The Way will forever change you.

By Little Paul Newton

Scripture quotations are from The Holy Bible, English Standard Version®, copyright © 2001 by Crossway Bibles, a publishing ministry of Good News Publishers. Used by permission. All rights reserved.

Copyright © 2021 by Robert Paul Newton

All rights reserved. No part of this publication may be reproduced, stored in a retrieval system, or transmitted in any form by any means, electronic, mechanical, photocopy, recording, or otherwise, without the prior permission of the author, except as provided for by USA copyright law.

Cover and interior design by Robert Paul Newton

The Lord of the Way once said,
"Foxes have holes, and birds of the air have nests,
but the Son of Man has nowhere to lay his head."
Thus, the Waytraveler likewise has no bed,
for they too are passing through to death.
Yet with death they will not dread
but will look forward to it instead.

Contents

	Introduction	7
1	God's Objectives	9
2	Receiving Salvation	22
3	Evidence of Salvation	39
4	The Pure of Heart	55
5	The Merciful Peacemaker	70
6	The Overcomers	86
7	The Prerequisite to Change	102

Introduction

I was one who saw and yet who did not see. At the early age of ten, I received Jesus Christ as my personal Lord and Savior and was baptized in a local Southern Baptist Church. In later years, I went to seminary and received a Master of Divinity at Southwestern Baptist Theological Seminary in Fort Worth, Texas. Afterwards, I served for about ten years as pastor for several Southern Baptist churches. Nonetheless, it was not until I embraced the truth found in this book when my life became profoundly changed. Although I had knowledge of it, and even thought I was living by it, I was not. But when my eyes became opened to the truth, and I fully embraced the Way of Christ, it was then when something amazing happened. It was then when sin lost its power over me, and I became free. Although temptation is still all around me, I no longer struggle with sin as I once did. Sin has simply lost its appeal.

Not only am I free from the power of sin, but I also feel different within. Even though for years I have felt God's presence in my life, it has now become increasingly stronger. It is as if I have become filled with his Spirit. This is not to say I have become saved, for I am fully persuaded I had already received the Holy Spirit based upon my faith in Jesus Christ. However, it was not until I began to follow the Way of Christ that my life became truly enriched by His peace and joy that I now experience.

With this being said, you may think you know the way of Christ. You may think you are following it, but you could be as I was. You could see, but then you do not see. What God has shown me may just possibly change your life as well. It is therefore my prayer for the Holy Spirit to impress upon you to read this book, and that he would also open your eyes to see and comprehend the complete and amazing value of his Way. These things must happen in order for you to experience the true power of the gospel of Jesus Christ and to walk in newness of life.

So, are you ready to begin?

1
God's Objectives

When it comes to writing about the Way of Christ, the most important place to begin is with the question, "What is God seeking to accomplish?" Some may reply that God is seeking to save a portion of humanity. They may even point to Jesus' statement in Luke 19:10 in which he said, **For the Son of Man came to seek and to save the lost.** If one did, they would be correct for this is God's primary objective. Yet, this raises another question, "Is God seeking to save just anyone who is lost or is he seeking to save only those in whom he has chosen?" This choosing of certain persons by God for salvation is referred to as the doctrine of predestination. Although this is scriptural, unfortunately there is a false teaching which can accompany it.

The False Teaching

What is this false teaching? It is to say that God has chosen certain people from humanity to be saved, and since he loves them unconditionally, they will be saved regardless of how they really live their lives, for after all, salvation is by grace through faith and is not of your own doing, it is a gift of God (Ephesians 2:8). So, in other words, this false belief causes one to believe that since salvation is not based upon one's works, when it comes to living righteously, all one must do is give it some effort. Then, no worries for they are the chosen ones.

Shockingly, this was the same mistake the Jews made during Jesus' time. Because they were Jews who had been given God's promise through Abraham and the Law through Moses, they believed they were automatically saved for they were God's chosen people. Yet, John the Baptist warned them in Matthew 3:7-10:

7 But when he saw many of the Pharisees and Sadducees coming to his baptism, he said to them, "You brood of vipers! Who warned you to flee from the wrath to come? 8 Bear fruit in keeping with repentance. 9 And do not presume to say to yourselves, 'We have Abraham as our father,' for I tell you, God is able from these stones to raise up children for Abraham. 10 Even now the axe is laid to the root of the trees. Every tree therefore that does not bear good fruit is cut down and thrown into the fire.

John the Baptist made it clear to them that even though they were the chosen ones, they still had to bear fruit in keeping with repentance. If they did not repent, then they would also suffer the wrath of God.

So, many people today are making this same mistake. Based upon their belief in the gospel, profession of faith, believer's baptism, and acceptance of this false teaching, they consider themselves as being automatically saved. And because of this, they will never seek repentance. They will go through life believing their salvation is secure, but unfortunately, they too will suffer the wrath of God.

The Necessity of Repentance

Now why is repentance necessary? The answer to this question is found in Jeremiah 31:31-34:

³¹ "Behold, the days are coming, declares the Lord, when I will make a new covenant with the house of Israel and the house of Judah, ³² not like the covenant that I made with their fathers on the day when I took them by the hand to bring them out of the land of Egypt, my covenant that they broke, though I was their husband, declares the Lord. ³³ But this is the covenant that I will make with the house of Israel after those days, declares the Lord: I will put my law within them, and I will write it on their hearts. And I will be their God, and they shall be my people. ³⁴ And no longer shall each one teach his neighbor and each his brother, saying, 'Know the Lord,' for they shall all know me, from the least of them to the greatest, declares the Lord. For I will forgive their iniquity, and I will remember their sin no more."

This passage is speaking of the new covenant in which God would make with Israel. The reason for this new covenant was because the children of Israel were unable to keep the law under the old covenant. So, in order to correct this, under the new covenant, God declared that he would put his law within his people by writing it upon their hearts. This implies repentance in that God's people would come to possess a higher level of admiration for his law, which then would result in a natural adherence to his commandments. And not only this but it also implies that God's people would come to have a close personal relationship with him, for they would all **'Know the Lord.'** It is therefore those who genuinely repent from the heart and who walk closely with him, who are God's people. It is they in whom God will forgive their iniquity and will remember their sin no more.

Yet how would God do this? In Ezekiel 36:27 one will read, **And I will put my Spirit within you, and cause you to walk in my statutes and be careful to obey my rules** (See Joel 2:28-29). Notice that God said he would accomplish his objective by placing his Spirit within his people. So, by the power of his indwelling Spirit, God would enable his people to naturally follow his Law. This knowledge of the necessity of one receiving the Holy Spirit is therefore essential to one understanding salvation.

Now returning to the doctrine of predestination, the chosen ones are therefore not those who believe and make a profession of faith. The chosen ones are those who believe and who have *received* the Holy Spirit! Once one has the Holy Spirit dwelling within them, it is they who will then have God's law written upon their hearts. It is they who will then repent and meet the expectations of God. And this will certainly happen for it is the Spirit of God who will ensure that it does.

To solidify the need for repentance even further one will also read in 2 Corinthians 6:16-18:

[16] **What agreement has the temple of God with idols? For we are the temple of the living God; as God said, "I will make my dwelling among them and walk among them,**

and I will be their God, and they shall be my people. **¹⁷ Therefore go out from their midst, and be separate from them, says the Lord, and touch no unclean thing; then I will welcome you, ¹⁸ and I will be a father to you, and you shall be sons and daughters to me, says the Lord Almighty."**

Notice in verse 17 that it is only *after* repentance when God will accept his people, for once they have separated themselves from all that is unclean, it is then when God will welcome them. But please keep in mind that salvation is both a "done deal" and a "not yet" concept. Now what do I mean by this? First, one will see in scripture that one will be saved at the moment they believe in the gospel of Jesus Christ and receive the Holy Spirit, for one will read in Romans 8:24, **For in this hope we were saved…** (See also Ephesians 2:5 & 8). Notice that Paul speaks of their salvation as being a done deal for they **were saved**. However, the one who receives the Holy Spirit is also a work in progress for one will also read in Philippians 2:12, **work out your own salvation with fear and trembling** (See also 1 Corinthians 1:18 & 15:2). So, what one is seeing in these passages is that when one receives the Holy Spirit they are saved at that moment, and the reason why this is true is because God does not fail. He will move them to repentance. He will sanctify them. Yet, the salvation process is not completed until the day of judgment, for that is when God will actually receive his people. But as one can also see from these and the previous passages, God is not only seeking to save certain individuals from the wrath to come, but he is also seeking to have them become separate from the world. They are to become holy as he is holy, **but as he who called you is holy, you also be holy in all your conduct** (1 Peter 1:15).

If these are the objectives of God, how then can people think they can live as they please? It is important for one to understand this important principle: *God does not fail.* His people will separate from the world. They will repent for he will make it so. Therefore, a profession of faith without repentance, is not good enough for it does not meet God's objective.

No doubt, there will be some who will object to what I have written declaring that one is saved by faith and not by works. Nonetheless, if all one has to do is make a profession of faith, then why do so many children do this, then later in life when they become truly saved, make another profession of faith? One may now claim that the children simply did not fully understand the gospel at the time, or they did what they did for the wrong reasons, such as they wanted to be like their peers. I would then say exactly! A profession of faith, by itself, is just spoken words. It is meaningless without the Holy Spirit. Yet, there are many who are resting the future of their eternal souls on the fact they have made a profession of faith and have been baptized.

Two Types of Followers

It is important for one to realize there are two types of followers. In John 15:2 Jesus said, **Every branch in me that does not bear fruit he takes away, and every branch that does bear fruit he prunes, that it may bear more fruit.** Notice how Jesus said, "in me." The branches of the vine therefore represent those *who claim* to follow him. One type of follower will claim to follow him but will not abide in his teachings. They will not live by Jesus' commandments. And as a result, their lives will be unfruitful. The second type of follower will also claim to follow Jesus and yet they will abide in his teachings. They will choose to live according to his commandments. And as a result, they will bear fruit. Because they bear fruit, the Father will then prune their hearts and lives so they will bear even more fruit. One will read in verse 8, **By this my Father is glorified, that you bear much fruit and so prove to be my disciples.** Notice that when one bears fruit, their fruit bearing *proves* they are indeed one of God's chosen people. So according to Jesus' teaching, one is maybe attached to him by a profession of faith, but if they do not abide in his word and produce fruit in keeping with repentance, then this is evidence that they do not have his Holy Presence flowing in their life. And because of this, they will be considered as a useless dead branch, which will then be thrown into the fire on the day of judgement (v. 6).

But this is not all for the Parable of the Weeds is yet another passage which reveals two types of followers. In Matthew 13:24-30, when Jesus was speaking to a large crowd, one will read:

24 He put another parable before them, saying, "The kingdom of heaven may be compared to a man who sowed good seed in his field, **25** but while his men were sleeping, his enemy came and sowed weeds among the wheat and went away. **26** So when the plants came up and bore grain, then the weeds appeared also. **27** And the servants of the master of the house came and said to him, 'Master, did you not sow good seed in your field? How then does it have weeds?' **28** He said to them, 'An enemy has done this.' So the servants said to him, 'Then do you want us to go and gather them?' **29** But he said, 'No, lest in gathering the weeds you root up the wheat along with them. ³⁰ Let both grow together until the harvest, and at harvest time I will tell the reapers, 'Gather the weeds first and bind them in bundles to be burned, but gather the wheat into my barn.'"

Since this parable confused Jesus' disciples, they then waited until later to ask him if he would explain it to them. In Matthew 13:37-42 one will then read:

³⁷ He answered, "The one who sows the good seed is the Son of Man. ³⁸ The field is the world, and the good seed is the sons of the kingdom. The weeds are the sons of the evil one, ³⁹ and the enemy who sowed them is the devil. The harvest is the close of the age, and the reapers are angels. ⁴⁰ Just as the weeds are gathered and burned with fire, so will it be at the close of the age. ⁴¹ The Son of Man will send his angels, and they will gather out of his kingdom all causes of sin and all law-breakers, ⁴² and throw them into the fiery furnace. In that place there will be weeping and gnashing of teeth.

In order to understand this parable, one must begin with the man who sows the good seed. The man was said to be the Son of Man, which represents Jesus, the Messiah. Thus, it was Jesus who sowed the good seed when he proclaimed the word of God. An example of this can be seen in Matthew 4:17, **From that time Jesus began to preach, saying, "Repent, for the kingdom of heaven is at hand."** And since the field represents the world (v. 38), Jesus' kingdom is therefore his church which he has planted in the world (16:18). This is seen by the fact that it is those who bore grain who are said to be sons of the kingdom (vv. 26 & 38). But Jesus also revealed that there were weeds which have come up *among* them. Thus, there are two types of believers within his church. But what is disturbing is that these weeds are said to have been planted by the devil! This then reveals that those who profess to believe in the gospel of Jesus Christ, but who refuse to repent, are in fact children of Satan. Though they may look like the children of God, and even believe that they are, they are in fact not, for God's people will bear fruit in keeping with repentance.

Are Your Works Good or Bad?

One may now point to the good things in which they have done for others and claim they have good works. With this in mind, let us now go to Matthew 7:21 for this verse, and the following verses, will reveal something important for us to understand. In Matthew 7:21, when speaking of the coming judgment of God, Jesus said, **Not everyone who says to me, 'Lord, Lord,' will enter the kingdom of heaven, but the one who does the will of my Father who is in heaven.** Once again Jesus revealed how there will be two types of followers, for one group will have done the Father's will while the other one had not. And though they may refer to him as Lord, those who did not do the Father's will, will be denied entrance into the kingdom of heaven. But this is not all, for Jesus then said in verses 22-23, **On that day many will say to me, 'Lord, Lord, did we not prophesy in your name, and cast out demons in your name, and do many mighty works in your name?' ^{23} And then will I declare to them, 'I never knew you; depart from me, you workers of lawlessness.'"** Here we see that those who referred to Jesus as Lord, but who did not do the Father's will and were denied entrance into the kingdom of heaven, also had a life filled with good works. And what is surprising is that some of them will have done many mighty works in Jesus' name. But nonetheless, Jesus said he would refer to them as being **workers of lawlessness**.

So, in order to understand why, one must look back to the preceding verses in which Jesus stated in Matthew 7:17-19:

[17] So, every healthy tree bears good fruit, but the diseased tree bears bad fruit. [18] A healthy tree cannot bear bad fruit, nor can a diseased tree bear good fruit. [19] Every tree that does not bear good fruit is cut down and thrown into the fire.

Although in this passage Jesus was speaking specifically of false prophets (teachers), it is really applicable to all who believe they are a child of God but who are not. Now in this passage Jesus revealed that it is possible for false believers to bear fruit or to do good deeds. However, notice that Jesus emphasized *good* fruit and *bad* fruit. So, even though some individuals will bear fruit, God will still consider them and their good works as being unacceptable for both them and their fruit are *diseased* (Matthew 12:33-37). What does this disease represent? It represents impure motives. In other words, their good deeds were not done in love but were simply done in order to benefit themselves. Thus, even though one may seem to be a good person who does good things for others, in God's eyes, they are still fruitless (1 Corinthians 13:1-7).

With this in mind, one may now be wondering how one can know for sure if they are truly saved? How can one know if they are a fruitful plant instead of a weed? How can one produce fruit with the right motives? The answer to these questions has already been given. One must receive the Spirit of God in which they will then walk in newness of life. Jesus told Nicodemus in John 3:5, **Truly, truly, I say to you, unless one is born of water and the Spirit, he cannot enter the kingdom of God.** One must therefore become born again.

The Apostle Paul also wrote in Romans 8:5-9:

⁵ For those who live according to the flesh set their minds on the things of the flesh, but those who live according to the Spirit set their minds on the things of the Spirit. ⁶ For to set the mind on the flesh is death, but to set the mind on the Spirit is life and peace. ⁷ For the mind that is set on the flesh is hostile to God, for it does not submit to God's law; indeed, it cannot. ⁸ Those who are in the flesh cannot please God. ⁹ You, however, are not in the flesh but in the Spirit, if in fact the Spirit of God dwells in you. Anyone who does not have the Spirit of Christ does not belong to him.

So as one can see, salvation is not about one making a profession of faith. It is not about one being baptized. Salvation is about one receiving the Holy Spirit. And when this takes place, the Spirit will then move them to repentance. He will then enable them to produce the good fruit God requires. They will become born again! However, this now raises another important question, "How does one receive the Holy Spirit?"

Summary Questions

1. What is God's primary objective?

2. What is the false teaching which deceives many?

3. Because of Israel's and Judah's disobedience, God declared he would make a new covenant with his people, one in which he would put his law within them by writing it upon their hearts, and they would all know him. In other words, God would cause his people to repent, but how would he do this?

4. This knowledge of the necessity of one receiving the Spirit is therefore essential to one understanding what?

5. The chosen ones are therefore not those who believe and make a profession of faith. The chosen ones are those who believe and who have *received* who?

6. When it comes to the saving of one of his chosen people, is it possible for God to fail?

7. According to Jesus' teachings there are two types of followers, one group is from him, and the other group is from Satan. So, how can one tell them apart?

8. Even though the lost can produce fruit, in God's eyes it is diseased, thus the fruit is not good. So, what does the disease represent?

9. According to Jesus, one must become what?

Notes

2
Receiving Salvation

The previous chapter ended with the question, "How does one receive the Holy Spirit?" To answer this question, one must turn to the nineteenth chapter of Acts in which the Apostle Paul runs into twelve men, who were disciples of John the Baptist. In verse 2 one will read, **And he said to them, "Did you receive the Holy Spirit when you believed?"** So, the answer then is that one becomes born again when one believes in the gospel of Jesus Christ. Yet, there is more.

The Spirit of Truth

Paul also wrote in Ephesians 1:13, **In him you also, when you heard the word of truth, the gospel of your salvation, and believed in him, were sealed with the promised Holy Spirit.** Paul emphasized that their receiving of the Holy Spirit was not based upon their belief in a gospel, but it was based upon their belief in a gospel that was also the word of truth. Since it is impossible for God to lie (Hebrews 6:18;

Titus 1:2), this then is only logical for God's Spirit would never be associated with a false gospel. So, in order to receive the Holy Spirit, one must believe in the *true* gospel of Jesus Christ.

But one's belief in the true gospel is not a *guarantee* that one has received the Holy Spirit. When preparing his disciples for when they would receive the Spirit at Pentecost, Jesus said in John 16:13, **When the Spirit of truth comes, he will guide you into all the truth, for he will not speak on his own authority…** Since one of the main purposes of the Holy Spirit is to guide God's people into all truth, and since God does not fail, one can then conclude that if one has received the Spirit of truth, who guides them, then one will continue to remain in the truth. They will not forsake the true gospel by accepting a false one. If one does, then the Holy Spirit was never with them, even though they had believed.

This then was why the apostles often warned church members to remain firmly established in their faith. An example of this is seen in 2 Thessalonians 2:15, **So then, brothers, stand firm and hold to the traditions that you were taught by us, either by our spoken word or by our letter.** (1 Corinthians 16:13; 2 Corinthians 1:24; Galatians 5:1; Ephesians 6:13; Philippians 4:1; Hebrews 3:14; Titus 1:9; and 1 Peter 5:9, 12) Since one's knowledge or understanding of scripture forms their beliefs, it then becomes essential to have and maintain the correct knowledge of scripture in order for one to receive salvation (Galatians 5:4; 1 Timothy 1:19). One will also read in Hebrews 3:14, **For we have come to share in Christ, if indeed we hold our original confidence firm to the end.** (Galatians 3:14; Mark 4:20; & 2 Corinthians 11:4). Now what is the true gospel? Does that mean one must believe *everything* correctly? No, but it does mean there are fundamental beliefs in which one cannot deny. Let me show you.

The Gospel Preached by Paul

When writing to the church in Corinth, the Apostle Paul listed several of these essential beliefs in 1 Corinthians 15:1-5:

¹ Now I would remind you, brothers, of the gospel I preached to you, which you received, in which you stand, ² and by which you are being saved, if you hold fast to the word I preached to you-unless you believed in vain. ³ For I delivered to you as of first importance what I also received: that Christ died for our sins in accordance with the Scriptures, ⁴ that he was buried, that he was raised on the third day in accordance with the Scriptures, ⁵ and that he appeared to Cephas, then to the twelve.

Notice how Paul appealed for them to remain in the gospel in which he had preached. He warned them that if they drifted away from his teachings, then their salvation would become uncertain. But what were those teachings? Paul began by first addressing the true identity of Jesus. Instead of writing Jesus Christ or Christ Jesus, he simply referred to Jesus as being "Christ." This was deliberate for Paul was emphasizing Jesus as being the promised Jewish Messiah (Acts 17:2-3). Then second, he stated how Christ's death was intentional in that Jesus was destined to die a sacrificial death on the cross for the sins of others. The death of Jesus was thus the fulfilment of God's saving plan for humanity for it fulfilled the Messianic prophecies found within Scripture. And then third, Paul stated how the Christ was buried and was raised again on the third day. The Messiah was not dead but had risen, according to Scripture, and there were eyewitnesses to this event. So, these are three fundamental beliefs in which one cannot deny. But there is much more that is implied, so let's take a closer look.

Jesus Is the Promised One

The first fundamental belief is a proper understanding of Jesus' identity. In Matthew 16:13-17 one will read:

¹³ Now when Jesus came into the district of Caesarea Philippi, he asked his disciple, "Who do people say that the Son of Man is?" ¹⁴ And they said, "Some say John the Baptist, others say Elijah, and others Jeremiah or one of the prophets." ¹⁵ He said to them, "But who do you say that I am?" ¹⁶ Simon Peter replied, "You are the Christ, the Son of the living God." ¹⁷ And Jesus answered him, "Blessed are you, Simon Bar-Jonah! For flesh and blood has not revealed this to you, but my Father who is in heaven.

When Jesus heard Peter's reply, he praised the Father for revealing this to Peter. Jesus was more than just a man, he was the Christ, the Son of God! When Peter called Jesus "the Christ" he was referring to Jesus as being the promised Messiah (John 1:41), but what exactly did this mean? In order to understand the full meaning of what Peter said, we must look at three other passages.

The first of the three passage is Genesis 17:4-8 in which God gave to Abraham two promises (or covenants).

⁴ "Behold, my covenant is with you, and you shall be the father of a multitude of nations. ⁵ No longer shall your name be called Abram, but your name shall be Abraham,

for I have made you the father of a multitude of nations. ⁶ I will make you exceedingly fruitful, and I will make you into nations, and kings shall come from you. ⁷ And I will establish my covenant between me and you and your offspring after you throughout their generations for an everlasting covenant, to be God to you and to your offspring after you. ⁸ And I will give to you and to your offspring after you the land of your sojournings, all the land of Canaan, for an everlasting possession, and I will be their God.

Now verses 4-7 represent the first promise from God and is the foundational covenant in which our salvation rests upon. So, God began by first promising Abraham he would become the father of a multitude of nations. God would make him into nations and kings would come from him. Since this did not happen physically, God was therefore speaking spiritually. But in order to understand what God was saying, one must keep in mind the following: First, God promised Abram, in Genesis 12:3 that in him (that is, in his Offspring not offspring, see Galatians 3:16) all the families of the earth would be blessed. Then second, because Abraham believed in God's promise, his faith was then counted to him as righteousness (Genesis 15:6). And this is the reason why salvation is by faith. Then third, since he was the first to believe in the promise, he then became the father of all who shares this faith in the promise, both Jew and Gentile (Romans 4:16). So, this was how God made Abraham the father of many nations. And this is how countless individuals throughout the world and age (the Church), who place their faith in Jesus Christ, the Offspring of Abraham, will enter the eternal kingdom of God.

Now the second promise (covenant) was physical for it was then when God promised Abraham in verse 8 that his future physical descendants would inherit the land around him, and that he would remain their God throughout the age. And it was then, in Genesis 17:9-14, when God made circumcision the sign, not for the first promise (or covenant) but for the second, which related specifically to Abraham and his physical offspring.

Turning now to the second messianic passage, which is found in 1 Chronicles 17:11-14 of when God spoke to David through the prophet Nathan, one will read:

[11] When your days are fulfilled to walk with your fathers, I will raise up your offspring after you, one of your own sons, and I will establish his kingdom. [12] He shall build a house for me, and I will establish his throne forever. [13] I will be to him a father, and he shall be to me a son. I will not take my steadfast love from him, as I took it from him who was before you, [14] but I will confirm him in my house and in my kingdom forever, and his throne shall be established forever.

God promised David that in the future he would raise up from his linage, which was the same as Abraham's, one who would be eternal. He would not only build a house for God, but his throne and kingdom would be established forever. And God would be to him a father and he would be to God a son.

With this being said, was it not Jesus in whom God raised up from the tomb? Yes it was, and which also confirmed him. And was it not Jesus who referred to God as being his Father and of himself as being God's Son (John 5:19-25)? Yes he did, very often. And was it not also Jesus who told his apostles he was going to prepare a place for them (John 14:2-3)? Yes he did, for the house in which he is preparing for them is the eternal house for God. It is the new Jerusalem in which one reads of in Revelations 21.

And turning now to Revelations 21, for it is the third messianic passage, since the first heaven and earth have passed away, John then sees the new Jerusalem coming down out of heaven from God and being forever joined with the new earth. One will read in Revelations 21:3, **And I heard a loud voice from the throne saying, "Behold, the dwelling place of God is with man. He will dwell with them, and they will be his people, and God himself will be with them as their God.** Notice how these words echo God's promise to Abraham. And as John looked upon the holy city, he then noticed specific details. For example, John observed how the city had a great high wall around it with twelve foundations, and upon these twelve foundations were written the names of the twelve apostles. Also, the twelve gates of the city were named according to the twelve tribes of Israel. The holy city is thus the eternal home of Israel! It is the place in which Jesus prepared for them. It is also the fulfillment of God's promise to David of an eternal Messiah, coming from his lineage, who would one eternal Sabbath day reign over his kingdom.

John's vision of the new Jerusalem was also the fulfilment of God's promise to Abraham, for John beheld the eternal Jewish home coming down to rest among the saved Gentile nations. Just as the eleven tribes surrounded Jerusalem, the saved Gentile nations will also surround the new Jerusalem in which they will walk by the light of God's glory, in which the kings of the nations will bring their glory into (v. 24). And just as the Levites were chosen by God from among the twelve tribes of Israel to serve him as temple priests in the earthly

Jerusalem, so has the saved Jewish nation been chosen from among the saved nations of the earth to serve God and the Lamb for all eternity (Revelations 22:3-4). So, they are truly a people who have been chosen and blessed by God. And as for us Gentiles, one should keep in mind that those living outside the city can enter the city at any time, for our names are written in the Lamb's book of life, and that living outside the city will be as living in the Garden of Eden. Thus, we will exist as God intended for us to exist from the beginning, which is to be caretakers of his creation. So as one can see, Abraham truly does become the father of a multitude of nations.

Returning to Peter's confession, one can now see the significance in what Peter said. Jesus is the Christ. And this belief is essential for salvation for the Apostle John wrote in 1 John 5:1, **Everyone who believes that Jesus is the Christ has been born of God…**

Now what you have just read is a good example of how one must believe in the fundamental truths of the gospel to be saved, and yet one does not have to believe *everything* correctly. Since there are other believers, who will have different opinions regarding the minor details I have just written, one of us, if not both, are wrong. Yet, since we both hold to Jesus as being the Christ, we are both still in the gospel of truth. This is because the Holy Spirit is guiding us into all truth (John 16:13). Thus, acquiring truth is a *process* in which we first begin with the fundamental truths.

Now returning to the fundamental beliefs, it is also important to realize that when one believes Jesus to be the promised Messiah, there are also two other beliefs which are to be understood. In the 1 Chronicles passage, the Messiah is said to be born from David's linage, which reveals his humanity. And then the Messiah is also said to be the eternal Son of God, which reveals his deity (Isaiah 9:6). Thus, the Messiah is both fully human and fully God.

With this in mind, the deity of Jesus is clearly seen in scripture, for in addition to the many miracles he performed, Jesus referred to God as being his Father. And because of this, the Jewish leaders sought to kill him for they understood Jesus to have made himself equal with God (John 5:18). Also, one will see in several places where Jesus was worshipped by others. Such a thing was unheard of by the Jews for this was reserved only for God (Matthew 28:17 & John 9:38). And yet, since Jesus allowed these individuals to worship him, he thus declared to the world he was indeed God in the flesh (John 20:28 & Matthew 1:23). And another example is seen in John 17:5, in which Jesus prayed to the Father saying, **And now Father, glorify me in your own presence with the glory that I had with you before the world existed.** Jesus' prayer reveals how he existed before creation, thus making him separate of creation and eternal. This is said of only three persons, the Father, the Son, and the Holy Spirit. Furthermore, in Colossians 1:16 Paul reveals Jesus to be the reason why creation even came into existence, **For by him all things were created, in heaven and on earth, visible and invisible, whether thrones or dominions or rulers or authorities-all things were created through him and for him.** Since it was for the Son's benefit in which the Father decided to create, creation is then a gift from the Father to the Son. So, if everything which was created was said to have been created by Jesus, through Jesus, and for Jesus, then Jesus could not have been created, as some believe. John states in 1 John 4:15, **Whoever confesses that Jesus is the Son of God, God abides in him, and he in God.**

Now that the deity of Jesus has been shown, scripture also reveals that he was fully human as well. One should keep in mind that Jesus' disciples walked with him and talked with him. They saw him hungry, thirsty, and weary. They saw him bleed. After spending as much time with him as they did, there was never any doubt in their minds concerning his humanity. Yet, in later years, John defended Jesus' humanity when he wrote in 2 John 7, **For many deceivers have gone out into the world, those who do not confess the coming of Jesus Christ in the flesh. Such a one is the deceiver and the antichrist.** Why is this important? In order for Jesus to substitute his life for ours, he had to be the same as us in every way. He had to be tempted as we are tempted, yet he was without sin. He had to feel pain as we feel pain, so he would suffer on the cross, as we would suffer. So, believing Jesus to have been fully human is also crucial to one walking in the truth.

Jesus Is the Only Lamb of God

The second fundamental belief is a proper understanding of what Jesus accomplished. In John 1:29, John the Baptist declared upon seeing Jesus, **…Behold, the Lamb of God, who takes away the sin of the world!** Jesus' death on the cross was the payment for the penalty for sin, the propitiation for all humanity (1 John 2:2). But why was it necessary for Jesus to have died for the sins of others? To answer this question, one must go back to the beginning of creation.

In the beginning, sin came into the world through Adam's disobedience. Then, in Genesis 5:1-3 one will read:

[1] This is the book of the generations of Adam. When God created man, he made him in the likeness of God. [2] Male and female he created them, and he blessed them and

named them Man when they were created. ³ **When Adam had lived 130 years, he fathered a son in his own likeness, after his image, and named him Seth.**

    Notice how the text began by stating Adam was created in the image of God. This statement was intended to be contrasted with the last statement in verse 3. In the last part of verse 3, one will read that Seth was not born in the image of God, but in the image of Adam. This reflects a change which had taken place within Adam. Even though Adam was first created in the perfect image of God, because of his disobedience, his image became no longer perfect. It became distorted by the sin he committed and by the spirit of sin which now dwelt within him. So, when Seth was born, he was not born in the image of the perfect God; he was born in the image of his imperfect father. This passage reveals how Seth inherited Adam's sinful nature (or better yet how the spirit of sin was passed onto him), and this happened without any sin being done by him (See Psalm 51:5). So, as a result of Adam's sin, death came upon all humanity for Adam's sinful nature (the spirit of sin) was allowed by God to be passed onto his descendants, and then to all future generations through the fathers (Leviticus 26:39). It was for this reason then that Jesus had to be conceived by the power of the Holy Spirit and not by an earthly father. By bypassing the curse, Jesus became as another Adam (1 Corinthians 15). So, as Adam was before the fall, so was Jesus.

    Since God allowed Adam's sinful nature to be passed onto his descendants, without them having to do any wrongful act to deserve it, God is now just in allowing Christ's perfect righteousness (for he was without sin) to be passed onto those who have done nothing righteous to earn it. Thus, due to Jesus' sacrificial death, his perfect righteousness can now be transferred to anyone in whom God chooses, and God chooses to give this special gift to those who believe and accept the gospel of his only Son.

Now in addition to this, believing Jesus to be the *only* eternal Son of God is also crucial to one remaining in the truth. One will read in John 3:16, **For God so loved the world, that he gave his only Son, that whoever believes in him should not perish but have eternal life.** (John 1:14; 3:18; & 1 John 4:9) So, those who believe that Satan is the brother of Jesus have denied a fundamental belief.

So, even if one may claim to adhere to the doctrine of salvation by grace, if they believe they have to be baptized, or they have to observe the Sabbath, or they have to speak in tongues, or they have to follow certain dietary restrictions, or they have to observe any other type of work in order to be saved, then they are not. They simply do not have the Spirit of truth within them. The Apostle Paul wrote in Galatians 5:4, **You are severed from Christ, you who would be justified by the law…** (or who would be justified by an act or deed).

Jesus Still Lives

Now the third essential belief is that Jesus rose again and is alive today. Since death is the consequence of sin, being without sin, Jesus' substitutional death on the cross condemned sin in his sinless flesh. His resurrection is therefore proof that God the Father has indeed accepted his Son's redeeming sacrifice. It is a declaration to the world that salvation has come to humanity and is *only* through Jesus Christ.

Yet, there are some who claim Jesus did not physically rise from the grave but rose as a spirit creature. They believe that only the spirit of the individual is raised. This too is not of the true gospel for Paul spoke in Romans 8:23 of how the apostles' longed for Jesus' return and wrote, **And not only the creation, but we ourselves, who have the firstfruits of the Spirit, groan inwardly as we wait eagerly for adoption as sons, the redemption of our bodies.** Notice how Paul specifically states they were waiting for the redemption of their *bodies*. Paul also states in 1 Corinthians 15:44, **It is sown a natural body; it is raised a spiritual body. If there is a natural body, there is also a spiritual body.** Yet, in either case, natural or spiritual, there is a body.

Also, when Jesus appeared to his disciples, he made every effort to prove he was not a spirit. In Luke 24:29-43 one will read:

[39] See my hands and my feet, that it is I myself. Touch me, and see. For a spirit does not have flesh and bones as you see that I have." [40] And when he had said this, he showed them his hands and his feet. [41] And while they still disbelieved for joy and were marveling, he said to them, "Have you anything here to eat?" [42] They gave him a piece of broiled fish, [43] and he took it and ate before them.

Notice how Jesus began by first asking his disciples to touch his hands and feet. Then in verse 41, Jesus asked for something to eat, in which he then eats a piece of broiled fish. All of this was intended to prove to them he was not a spirit.

Yet, there are some who claim that a spirit can materialize for a brief time and take on physical properties. Thus, they will focus on the aspect of the passage in which Jesus ate and was touched. They may then point to Geneses 18 in which the Lord and two other angels appeared to Abraham, just before Sodom and Gomorrah were destroyed. In this account, one will read in verse 8 of how the Lord and the two angels ate a meal in which Abraham prepared. They will claim how this proves that angels (spirits) can be touched and can also eat. The fact that a spirit can eat and be touched is not denied. But they fail to see the greatest evidence of all which proves that Jesus was not a spirit. They fail to see that the main reason Jesus asked his disciples to touch him was so that they could see he had a body of *flesh* and *bones*. Jesus stated **Touch me, and see. For a spirit does not have flesh and bones as you see that I have.** Thus, Jesus made it perfectly clear to his disciples that he was not a spirit but that he had indeed risen from the grave with an eternal physical body.

Yet, our new bodies will have a spiritual aspect to them, for not only does Paul refer to the raised new body as being spiritual (1 Corinthians 15:44) but notice how there was no mention of blood in Luke's passage, for Jesus only says his body was of flesh and bones. Paul wrote in 1 Corinthians 15:50, **I tell you this, brothers: flesh and blood cannot inherit the kingdom of God, nor does the perishable inherit the imperishable.** Since Jesus did not mention blood, this reveals the eternal spiritual nature of his physical body. With our present physical body, the life is in the blood (Leviticus 17:11), but in the new spiritual body, the life is in the Spirit. Paul wrote in Romans 8:11, **If the Spirit of him who raised Jesus from the dead dwells in you, he who raised Christ Jesus from the dead will also give life to your mortal bodies through his Spirit who dwells in you.** Our bodies are not forsaken but God will give them eternal life through his indwelling Spirit. And when that day comes, we will become like our Savior. We will have bodies of flesh and bone and we will live eternally in his kingdom by the power of his indwelling Spirit.

Although disagreements on the minor details are expected, these are the essential beliefs in which one must embrace for salvation: Jesus, the only Son of God, became the Christ, thus he was fully God and fully human. Jesus was also sinless who died a sacrificial death in order to pay the penalty for our sins, and on the third day, was raised to life with an eternal physical body. All of which was in accordance with Scriptures. This is the true gospel of Jesus Christ, and according to God's promise, this is what one must believe in order to receive his Spirit. But belief in the true gospel alone is not enough to confirm, without a doubt, that one has become reborn, for it must be followed by yet another sign.

Summary Questions

1. How does one receive the Holy Spirit?

2. One's belief in the true gospel of Jesus Christ is not a _____ that one has received the Holy Spirit?

3. If one forsakes the true gospel by accepting a false one, what does this mean?

RECEIVING SALVATION

4. The first fundamental belief is a proper understanding of Jesus' identity.
    a. He was the _____ which means he was the fulfilment of God's promise to Abraham and David.
    b. Jesus was therefore fully _____ and fully _____.
    c. Also, he is the only _____ of God.

5. The second fundamental belief is a proper understanding of what Jesus accomplished.
    a. Jesus was without _____ in that he kept God's laws perfectly.
    b. Thus, he did not have to die, but chose to die a _____ death to save us from the penalty of our sins.

6. And the third fundamental belief is that Jesus rose again on the third day with an eternal _____ body and is alive today.

7. Acquiring truth is a _____ in which we first begin with the fundamental truths and then grow in our knowledge and understanding. Because of this, it is okay if we disagree on minor details.

THE WAYTRAVELERS

Notes

3
Evidence of Salvation

In the previous chapter it was shown that one receives the Holy Spirit by faith in the true gospel of Jesus Christ, and when one continues to reside in the truth, these two things then become signs of one who has truly received the Spirit of God. However, there is yet another sign. So, now the question is this, "What is the third sign?" The answer is repentance. And even though the necessity of repentance was covered to some extent in chapter one, there is still much more to be learned.

Why Is Repentance a Sign?

To begin with, one will read in Matthew 4:17, **From that time Jesus began to preach, saying, "Repent, for the kingdom of heaven is at hand."** Here one sees Jesus, at the beginning of his ministry, proclaiming to the people how they *must* repent. They must forsake their sinful behavior and turn to God. Since John the Baptist prepared the way for the Lord, some may claim that Jesus was simply using John's rhetoric in order to reveal to the people his connection to John, for John preached repentance and his baptism was a baptism of repentance. However, this is not the only time in which Jesus taught the necessity of repentance.

When nearing the end of his ministry, Jesus spoke of a tragic event and said in Luke 13:3, **No, I tell you; but unless you repent, you will all likewise perish.** Jesus' words are clear. Repentance is necessary for salvation. If one does not repent, then they will perish regardless of what they profess to believe. One will also read in Luke 24:45-47 of when Jesus appeared to his disciples soon after he rose from the grave:

[45] Then he opened their minds to understand the Scriptures, [46] and said to them, "Thus it is written, that the Christ should suffer and on the third day rise from the dead, [47] and that repentance and forgiveness of sins should be proclaimed in his name to all nations, beginning from Jerusalem.

Here one sees Jesus commissioning his disciples to take the gospel to the nations. But notice how he told them that repentance and forgiveness of sins were to be preached in his name. This is to say that the disciples were to preach to the nations of God's coming wrath and that the only way to escape God's wrath was for one to repent, which is to change the way they lived and begin living according to Christ's way, and then God would forgive them of their sins. This is quite different from passages such as Mark 16:16; Luke 8:12; John 3:16; 8:24; and 11:25-26 in which all one has to do is believe in Jesus (the gospel) and they will be saved from God's wrath. One may now wonder if there is a conflict between these passages, and the answer is "no." This is because once again when one receives the Spirit of God by faith (or belief), one will then repent, for God's Spirit will *cause* them to repent (Ezekiel 36:27). Since God does not fail, if one does not repent, then one has simply not received the Spirit of God. So, with this in mind, even though Jesus taught that belief in him was necessary for salvation, in this passage, Jesus was merely emphasizing to his disciples that one's belief in him must result in repentance in order for individuals to receive God's forgiveness.

To further support this point, in all of Jesus' teachings concerning the coming judgment of God, not one of them shows God's judgment being based solely upon what one claimed to believe. Instead, they are based upon what one did in this life as *a result* of what they believed. An example of this can be seen in Matthew 7:24-27:

²⁴ "Everyone then who hears these words of mine and does them will be like a wise man who built his house on the rock. ²⁵ And the rain fell, and the floods came, and the winds blew and beat on that house, but it did not fall, because it had been founded on the rock. ²⁶ And everyone who hears these words of mine and does not do them will be like a foolish man who built his house on the sand. ²⁷ And the rain fell, and the floods came, and the winds blew and beat against that house, and it fell, and great was the fall of it."

These words of Jesus, who would one day be the judge of humanity, were meant to emphasize the importance of one obeying him. If one lives their life according to his teachings, they will then survive the coming storm of God's wrath.

Another example is seen in Matthew 25:31-46 in which Jesus revealed that on judgment day, as a shepherd who separates the sheep from the goats, he will also separate the people of the nations into two groups. Jesus will then say to those whom he considers as being sheep:

³⁴ …'Come, you who are blessed by my Father, inherit the kingdom prepared for you from the foundation of the world. ³⁵ For I was hungry and you gave me food, I was thirsty and you gave me drink, I was a stranger and you welcomed me, ³⁶ I was naked and you clothed me, I was sick and you visited me, I was in prison and you came to me.' (vv. 34-36)

But as for those whom he considers as being goats, even though they too will refer to him as Lord, they will be denied entrance into the kingdom. They will be denied for they had not done these things for others.

So, as one can see, Jesus taught from the beginning to the end of his ministry that one must not only believe but also repent in order to receive salvation (Hebrews 5:9). But please keep in mind that repentance should not be viewed as a work which must be done in order for one to receive salvation, it is simply the result of one having already received salvation (the Spirit) by faith. *Thus, genuine repentance is impossible without him.*

Now does this conflict with the teachings of the apostles, no it does not, for the Apostle Paul wrote in 2 Thessalonians 1:6-8:

⁶ since indeed God considers it just to repay with affliction those who afflict you, ⁷ and to grant relief to you who are afflicted as well as to us, when the Lord Jesus is revealed from heaven with his mighty angels ⁸ in flaming fire, in-

flicting vengeance on those who do not know God and on those who do not obey the gospel of our Lord Jesus.

Paul clearly states that those who are saved from God's coming wrath are not those who believe in the gospel but are those who believe and obey the gospel. To support this even further, in Acts chapter seventeen, Paul addresses the men of Athens, the Areopagus, and says in verses 30-31, **The times of ignorance God overlooked, but now he commands all people everywhere to repent, ^{31} because he has fixed a day on which he will judge the world in righteousness by a man who he has appointed…** Notice how Paul does not say that God commands people everywhere to believe in the gospel. He says that God commands people everywhere *to repent*. Thus, Paul would not have stated it this way unless he believed repentance was also necessary for salvation.

This is also supported by the Apostle John who wrote in 1 John 3:10, **By this it is evident who are the children of God, and who are the children of the devil: whoever does not practice righteousness is not of God, nor is the one who does not love his brother.** John' words are clear. If one does not practice righteousness, they are not a child of God. If one does not walk in love towards others, then they belong to the devil.

So as one can see, the necessity of repentance is taught by both Jesus and his apostles. Since this is the case, one may now wonder why many churches today are not emphasizing this? And I believe the answer is because many people simply do not understand what true repentance is. In other words, when people think of repentance, they think of one living by a set of rules and thus they reject it for this is a works-based salvation. But I will soon show that repentance is not about following a set of rules; it is about following *a way of life*. And when one genuinely repents, it is then when one will experience the gospel's true power.

The Gospel's True Power

Just before Jesus was arrested, he spoke with his disciples and said in John 14:15-16, **If you love me, you will keep my commandments. ¹⁶ And I will ask the Father, and he will give you another Helper, to be with you forever…** Jesus was clearly speaking of a time period after his death, resurrection, and ascension, which we know now to be the day of Pentecost. Jesus promised his disciples he would give them a Helper, which is the Holy Spirit, and he would never leave them but would forever remain with them. Jesus then says in verse 17, **even the Spirit of truth, whom the world cannot receive, because it neither sees him nor knows him. You know him, for he dwells with you and will be in you.** Although this verse was looked at in the previous chapter, I would like to now point out that the Spirit had been with the disciples, for Jesus clearly said, "he dwells *with* you." Evidence of this can be seen in that Jesus' true identity was made known to them. However, Jesus informed them that the location of the Holy Spirit would soon change, for on the day of Pentecost the Spirit would move from being *with* them to being *in* them.

Because of Jesus' statement, I have come to believe the following: First, one receives the Spirit at the time of one's belief in the gospel of Jesus Christ, for once again one will read in Galatians 3:14, **so that in Christ Jesus the blessing of Abraham might come to the Gentiles, so that we might receive the promised Spirit through faith.** Thus, the Spirit of

God will move from coming and going in one's life, for he has been cultivating their heart, to remaining *with* them. Then second, the Spirit's presence with one becomes permanent for one will read in Ephesians 1:13, **In him you also, when you heard the word of truth, the gospel of your salvation, and believed in him, were sealed with the promised Holy Spirit…** (John 10:28-29). Then third, once one receives the Holy Spirit by faith and becomes permanently sealed, it is then when the Spirit will guide them to true repentance. And when this occurs, it is then when the Holy Spirit will move from being *with* them to being *in* them.

This may sound strange at first, but consider this for a moment, are people not often led by others to say this in their prayer when they receive the gospel of Jesus Christ, "Lord please come into my *heart* and *life*…?" I believe this is not by chance, but this phrase has come about by those who have held to this same conviction as I in that there is a distinction between one having the Spirit in one's life by faith and then having the Spirit in one's heart when one repents and walks in love.

Now what is interesting about this, as Jesus pointed out to Nicodemus, is that this process is similar to the worldly birthing process. For instance, as with any pregnancy, once a woman becomes pregnant, they cannot become unpregnant for the natural process will result with a child being born. And this is also true of the spiritual process, for what God begins within a person he will see through to its completion. And in addition to this, the actual birthing process is not complete until one comes forth out of the womb. Thus, one's birthday is not when one was conceived but when one comes into the world. This same concept is also true of those who believe in the gospel of Jesus Christ, but who have yet to learn of the way of love.

Because of their faith, that individual *is now saved* for the Spirit will never leave them nor forsake them. And since the seed of faith has been planted within them, the Holy Spirit will oversee the maturing process of that seed. He will guide them to repentance. And once their faith becomes fully mature and they begin to abide in love, it is then, at that moment when they will move forth from the womb. It is then when they will truly become born again and will walk in newness of life.

What I have just described is supported by the Apostle John who wrote in 1 John 4:16…**God is love, and whoever abides in love abides in God, and God abides in him.** Notice that God is love and thus his Spirit is a Spirit of love, and when one abides in love, one is actually abiding in God. They are abiding in his Spirit! And John then states that God (or his Spirit) is abiding *in* them. So, when one believes in the gospel of Jesus Christ, and then repents by putting on love (Colossians 3:14), it is then when the Holy Spirit will move into their heart. It is then when God will begin to abide *in* them. *And this is the evidence or proof that one has indeed received the Holy Spirit*, for one will also read in 1 John 4:7, **Beloved, let us love one another, for love is from God, and whoever loves has been born of God and knows God.**

So, when one repents, by abiding in love and then walking in love, it is then when one's faith becomes complete. This was why James wrote in 2:22, **You see that faith was active along with his works, and faith was completed by his works.** And to confirm that James was actually speaking of works done in love, James wrote in 2:12, **So speak and so act as those who are to be judged under the law of liberty.** But please keep in mind that the law of liberty was simply another way of referring to the second great commandment, for one will read in James 2:8, **If you really fulfill the royal law**

according to the Scriptures, "You shall love your neighbor as yourself," you are doing well. So, when James speaks of works completing one's faith, he is actually saying that when one walks in love, it is then when their loving words and actions will complete their faith. James therefore taught that one must walk by both faith and love for faith without works (works of love) is dead (James 2:17). This too is supported by the Apostle Paul who wrote in Galatians 5:6, **For in Christ Jesus neither circumcision nor uncircumcision counts for anything, but only faith working through love.**

Love Fulfills the Law

Another reason why abiding and walking in love is so important is that it is love which fulfills the law. In Matthew 22:37-39 one will read of when a lawyer tests Jesus by asking him which commandment of the Law is the greatest:

[37] **And he said to him, "You shall love the Lord your God with all your heart and with all your soul and with all your mind. [38] This is the great and first commandment. [39] And a second is like it: You shall love your neighbor as yourself.**

Notice that both commandments speak of one abiding in love. The first is for one to love God with a dominant love, and the second is for one to love others. Jesus then said in verse 40, **On these two commandments depend all the Law and the Prophets.** This is to say that the entire Jewish scriptures rested upon love. Therefore, if one were to abide in love and then to walk in love towards God and others, they would then meet the demands of the Law. The Apostle Paul later wrote in Romans 13: 9-10:

⁹ For the commandments, "You shall not commit adultery, You shall not murder, You shall not steal, You shall not covet," and any other commandment, are summed up in this word: "You shall love your neighbor as yourself." ¹⁰ Love does no wrong to a neighbor; therefore, love is the fulfilling of the law.

But in addition to these two commandments, John revealed a third in 1 John 3:23, **And this is his commandment, that we believe in the name of his Son Jesus Christ and love one another...** Notice how the third commandment is combined with one of the previous two commandments. This was intended to show how this commandment belonged with the other two. Also notice how one is to believe and the other one is to love. Once again one sees faith and love being placed together in order for one to receive salvation. *Thus, love by itself is nothing without faith in Jesus Christ, and faith in Jesus Christ by itself is nothing unless one abides in love.* So, the third commandment is for one to believe in the name of Jesus, which is to say one is to believe in the fundamental beliefs of the true revelation of Jesus Christ (John 12:36; 14:1; & 16:27). John wrote in 1 John 3:24, **Whoever keeps his commandments abides in God, and God in him...**

Now it is these three commandments which define the Way of Christ, for they came about as a result of Jesus teaching the necessity of one living by them (John 13:34-35; 14:15-24; & 15:1-17). And within time, they not only began to be considered as summary commandments that defined the Way (Acts 18:25-26; 19:9, & 23), but they also began to be viewed as a law themselves. James referred to the second commandment as the perfect law, a law of liberty, and a royal law (James 1:25 & 2:8), and Paul referred to it as the law of Christ (Galatians 6:2). So, as one can see, one is no longer to obey the letter of the law for salvation, but instead one is to be led by the law of love, the divine nature of God, for one will read in Romans 8:14, **For all who are led by the Spirit of God are sons of God.**

How God's People Will Be Judged

Now that one understands that love fulfills the righteous requirement of the law, let us once again look at the coming judgement of God. Yet, this time let us look at it regarding how important it will be for the children of God to have walked in love. With this in mind, the best place to begin is in Revelations 20:11-12 in which one will read:

¹¹ Then I saw a great white throne and him who was seated on it. From his presence earth and sky fled away, and no place was found for them. ¹² And I saw the dead, great and small, standing before the throne, and books were opened. Then another book was opened, which is the book of life. And the dead were judged by what was written in the books, according to what they had done.

In God's revelation given to the Apostle John, he sees God setting on his thrown and the earth and sky are removed. Then all of humanity will stand before him to be judged according to what has been written in books. In other words, everyone's name is found in a book and under their name is recorded everything they have said and done. Then out of the many books in which John sees, he notices a special book. It is special for it contains the names of all those who are to be saved. It is the book of life.

Let's now take a closer look at the judgement of those found in the book of life. James revealed in 2:12 that the children of God will be judged under the law of liberty. He writes, **So speak and so act as those who are to be judged under the law of liberty**. Once again, he was referring to the second great commandment (James 2:8). So, James revealed that everything, which is said and done, by the child of God, will be judged by the law of love and not the written Law.

But since the child of God is now judged by love, they are held to a higher accountability. This is seen in 1 Corinthians 13:1-3 in which the Apostle Paul writes:

[1] If I speak in the tongues of men and of angels, but have not love, I am a noisy gong or a clanging cymbal. [2] And if I have prophetic powers, and understand all mysteries and all knowledge, and if I have all faith, so as to remove mountains, but have not love, I am nothing. [3] If I give away all I have, and if I deliver up my body to be burned, but have not love, I gain nothing.

So, everything said and done must be done in love. Anything which is not done in love is done in vain. Love has therefore become the standard by which the child of God is to live by and is what they will be judged by. And this actual judgement process can be seen in 1 Corinthians 3:12-15 in which Paul writes:

[12] Now if anyone builds on the foundation with gold, silver, precious stones, wood, hay, straw- [13] each one's

works will become manifest, for the Day will disclose it, because it will be revealed by fire, and the fire will test what sort of work each one has done. **¹⁴ If the work that anyone has built on the foundation survives, he will receive a reward. ¹⁵ If anyone's work is burned up, he will suffer loss, though he himself will be saved, but only as through fire.**

When this text is viewed with the previous passages, one's loving acts of kindness are represented as gold, silver, and precious stones. And once again, when God's people are judged by the law of love, only those things which are done in love will survive.

So now we know that in order for one to be saved one must receive the Spirit by faith in the true gospel of Jesus Christ. And when one receives the Spirit, one will repent by abiding and walking in love, for the Spirit will ensure they do. This then becomes not only true repentance but also a sign of true salvation.

Now with this in mind, it is troubling that many today, though they hold firmly to being saved by grace, are living by a set of rules instead of the law of love. What are these rules? They will attend church regularly. They will tithe faithfully. They will be actively involved in church. They will not use foul language. They will not gamble. They will not drink. They will not smoke. They will not have premarital sex. They will not lie, and they will not steal. Although most of these are biblical, one's adherence to these is not true repentance. One could say that these rules have become the ten commandments for evangelicals and have become the defining guidelines of what it means to be a good Christian, a true Christian. Nevertheless, if one does not abide and walk in love, but instead relies upon these things, then they too will be rejected by God. One simply cannot reject the Way without also rejecting the Author of the Way. Therefore, believing and remaining in the true gospel and repenting by walking in love and truth are the true signs of salvation, and it is not speaking in tongues, receiving baptism by water, making a profession of faith, or living by the evangelical ten commandments. As John says in 1 John 4:8, **Anyone who does not love does not know God because God is love.**

Summary Questions

1. Three signs that one has received the Holy Spirit is belief in the true gospel, continuation in the true gospel, and _____.

2. Repentance is necessary for salvation, for if one does not repent, then they will _____ regardless of what they profess to believe.

3. Repentance should not be viewed as a work which must be done in order for one to receive salvation, it is simply the _____ of one having already received salvation (the Holy Spirit) by faith.

4. True repentance is not about following a set of rules; it is about following a _____ of _____.

EVIDENCE OF SALVATION

5. The three stages of the Holy Spirit.
    a. First, the Spirit comes and goes in one's life as he _____ their heart.
    b. Then second, upon one's belief in the true gospel of Jesus Christ, the Spirit then permanently _____ them by reaming with them.
    c. Then third, the Spirit guides them to true repentance, and when this occurs, it is then when the Spirit will move from being _____ them to being _____ them.

6. Why is it that when one abides in love, one is actually abiding in God's Spirit and God's Spirit is abiding *in* them?

7. Why is love nothing without faith in Jesus Christ, and faith in Jesus Christ is nothing unless one abides in love?

8. Love is therefore the standard by which the child of God is to _____ by and is what they will be _____ by.

Notes

4
The Pure in Heart

Since it has been shown that true repentance is to abide and to walk in truth and love, the questions are now, "What is love and how does one actually abide in love? Some may think these questions are silly, but in my case, I did not fully understand the biblical meaning of the word "love." With my blue-collar upbringing and with the years I spent in the Marine Corp infantry, when I first heard of one walking in love, I pictured in my mind someone who was all sweat and cuddly going around hugging everyone they met. Then later I learned it meant more of a brotherly love, and this was what I believed for years. But this was still not totally correct. So, what does it mean to love others?

The Biblical Meaning of Love

In Matthew 7:12, Jesus defined love when he said, **So whatever you wish that others would do to you, do also to them, for this is the Law and the Prophets.** To love others then is to simply treat others the way you would like to be treated. It is to value others and to care for them just as you value and care for yourself. And it is from this principle that Paul later built upon when he wrote, in Galatians 5:23, that love is patient, kind, good, faithful, gentle, and self-controlled, and then in 1 Corinthians 13:4-5 he wrote that love does not envy, boast or insist on its own way. It is not arrogant, rude, irritable, or resentful. All these things, which Paul listed, can be obtained by simply asking oneself, "How would I like to be treated?" So, it is this natural internal moral law which serves to give one the basic knowledge or understanding of what love is, and it is this inward moral law that exists in all people, for all individuals are created in the image of a loving God.

Yet, we need to keep in mind that this image of ours is now distorted by sin. Though we may possess this inner moral law, we can still choose to ignore it, and over time, even become callused to its existence. But deep down within us, we still know when we have done something wrong to another simply because we would not have wanted it done to us.

Abiding in Love

Turning now to the second question of how one can abide in love, the answer we seek is also found in Jesus' Sermon on the Mount. Now within Jesus' sermon, he gave three characteristics which define what it means to be a child of God, and one of those characteristics gives us the solution. Jesus said in Matthew 5:8, **Blessed are the pure in heart, for they shall see God.** *So, to abide in love means for one to have and to maintain a heart that is pure.* But how does having a pure heart enable one to abide in love? In Matthew 15:19 Jesus taught, **For out of the**

heart come evil thoughts, murder, adultery, sexual immorality, theft, false witness, slander. Since the heart represents that portion within our inner being which houses our emotions, it is therefore certain emotions within us which are evil. And it is these evil emotions which then produce evil thoughts, which then lead us to doing and saying evil things. So, in order for us to treat others as we would want to be treated, we must learn how to control or to purge ourselves of these emotions.

With this in mind, Jesus then revealed that the first emotion of the heart, in which one must control, is one's anger. Though anger is a natural emotion, if not handled properly, one's anger could lead one into sin. In Matthew 5:21-22 Jesus said:

21 "You have heard that it was said to those of old, 'You shall not murder; and whoever murders will be liable to judgment.' 22 But I say to you that everyone who is angry with his brother will be liable to judgment; whoever insults his brother will be liable to the council; and whoever says, 'You fool!' will be liable to the hell of fire.

Jesus taught that when one becomes angry with another, they have become liable to judgment. This is not to say they have committed a sin, but simply that they are now standing on dangerous ground. Why is this? If one is not careful, for it can happen quickly, one's anger towards another could turn to bitterness, thus causing them to say a negative remark or insult towards the person. If this happened, Jesus said they would then be blameworthy enough to be judged by the council, which was the Sanhedrin or the Jewish court. In other words, they had become guilty enough to be judged by man. But then, if one's bitterness towards another turned to hate causing them to say, "you fool," they have crossed the line. They crossed the line because they acted out of hate, for the intention of the name calling was to hurt the person. Jesus then said they would **be liable to the hell of fire** (Matthew 12:36-37). They would be blameworthy enough to be judged by God.

So, within this passage, Jesus revealed two important principles. First is that a progression takes place within one's heart. If one's anger is not kept in check, then it will eventually lead to bitterness, and then to hate. Then second, though the person did not actually commit murder, they were still guilty before God simply because they insulted another person out of hate. The Apostle John wrote in 1 John 3:15, **Everyone who hates his brother is a murderer, and you know that no murderer has eternal life abiding in him.** It is therefore the act of hating others which will condemn one to hell, and anything which comes out of hate is equal to murder. Murder is merely the greatest expression of hate.

Since anger has the potential to turn into bitterness, it is only logical then for one to avoid it completely. But as stated earlier, anger is a natural emotion, so this would be impossible. Because of this, Paul taught that the best way to deal with one's anger was to deal with it immediately. He wrote in Ephesians 4:26, **Be angry and do not sin; do not let the sun go down on your anger…** So, when one becomes angry with another, they are to go at once to the individual and work it out.

But how exactly does one remove such a strong emotion as anger from one's heart? This is done in just a few steps. First, in moments of anger, we must remind ourselves of who we truly are. We must remind ourselves that we too have offended others. We must remind ourselves that we too have hurt others with our words or actions. What this does is that it causes us to relate to the one who has just offended us. Once we begin to relate to them, it is then when the storm of anger within us will begin to diminish, and we can then speak with them calmly.

Now what I have just shared with you can change your life. It is that *your thoughts affect your emotions.* If you focus your thoughts on the wrong done to you, then your anger towards your offender will intensify. But if you focus your thoughts on your own mistakes, your anger will begin to dissipate. So, what one sees taking place is that the mind can actually guide one's heart. Just as the small rudder on the back of a large sailing vessel can turn the vessel, and within time, can even turn the vessel completely around, so can one's mind turn one's heart around. Therefore, by forcing yourself to think a certain way; you can actually change how you are feeling. You can actually control your emotions. This is how you can abide in love. This is how you can navigate your heart through the emotional storms of your day.

And once you have removed the storm of anger from your heart and have spoken with them, the next step is then made possible which is to forgive them. Forgiveness is simply an act of mercy in which one chooses not to hold the person's mistake against them. Now consider this, how can one be angry with another when they too are guilty of similar offenses? One will read in Matthew 6:14-15 where Jesus taught, **For if you forgive others their trespasses, your heavenly Father will also forgive you, ¹⁵ but if you do not forgive others their trespasses, neither will your Father forgive your trespasses.** Since everyone is guilty of their own trespasses, one *must* therefore forgive others in order to be forgiven by God. Having a merciful spirit thus becomes another sign of one who has the Spirit within them. So, if one chooses to hate another, then the Spirit of God cannot be in their heart, and if one refuses to change but instead chooses to continue to hate another, then the Holy Spirit was never with them.

I fully understand how difficult it can be to forgive others, and for those who have experienced horrific offenses, this may seem impossible. With this being said, some offenses will take more time than others to work through. Nevertheless, when one has experienced the forgiveness and mercy of God for their sins and have felt the warmth of his presence in their life, they will not let anger, bitterness, or hate ruin that for them. So, for the child of God, their love of God will prevail. This is why one must love God above everything, including their hurt feelings and the resentment they may have towards another.

Then the final step is found in Matthew 5:44, **But I say to you, Love your enemies and pray for those who persecute you...** Here is the radical love to which God's people are called to live. We are to love our enemies. We are to love those who wish us harm. This is nothing short of complete insanity in the eyes of the world. Yet, this is what it means to abide in love. Notice that Jesus tells his followers to pray for those who persecute them. Why prayer? Praying for one's enemies is the equal and opposite reaction to persecution. It is the child of God matching the same intensity of darkness with the same intensity of light by asking their heavenly Father to bless their enemies instead of holding their offences against them.

But there is still more for one will also read in Romans 12:19-21:

[19] **Beloved, never avenge yourselves, but leave it to the wrath of God, for it is written, "Vengeance is mine, I will repay, says the Lord."** [20] **To the contrary, "if your enemy is hungry, feed him; if he is thirsty, give him something to**

drink; for by so doing you will heap burning coals on his head." ²¹ **Do not be overcome by evil, but overcome evil with good.**

In this passage, the Apostle Paul reveals how we are at war with the evil around us. Just as there are casualties of war, the children of God will also suffer loss. However, when we are assaulted by another, we are to respond by doing good things for them, and in so doing, our good deeds will be as a heap of burning coals placed upon their heads. But we must do so with this in mind; we are not at war with the people, we are at war with the evil within them. Thus, the reason we do good things for them is not to torture them, but it is to seek to save the pawn of evil from eternal destruction. Let us therefore seek to save the souls of our offenders. Let our hearts mourn for them knowing that if we are unsuccessful, they will one day fall into the hands of an angry God. By choosing to see things from this perspective, we will soon find that our own hurt feelings will have dissipated.

Turning now to lust, just as it is natural for one to become angry, it is also natural for one to find others physically attractive. Yet, as with anger, if one's physical attraction for another is not managed properly, it could turn into something else. One will read in Matthew 5:27-28, **"You have heard that it was said, 'You shall not commit adultery.'** [28] **But I say to you that everyone who looks at a woman with lustful intent has already committed adultery with her in his heart.**

In this passage, Jesus was speaking against married men who, upon seeing an attractive woman, would allow lust to enter their heart. Since lust leads to sexual immorality, just as bitterness leads to hate, some men would then become led to devise plans on how they could have sexual relations with the woman. When this took place, because of their intent, they had just entered into sexual immorality. So, even though they had not actually committed the physical act of adultery, Jesus showed that in God's eyes, they were still guilty of the sin (1 Corinthians 6:9-10). Therefore, just as with hate and murder, any word or action which comes from sexual immorality is equal to the actual act of adultery, for adultery simply represents the greatest expression of the sin.

So, how can one prevent lust from developing within one's heart? The process for avoiding lust can be learned from the incident that happened between Joseph and Potiphar's wife. In Genesis 39:8-9 one will read of how Potiphar's wife tried to seduce Joseph:

8 But he refused and said to his master's wife, "Behold, because of me my master has no concern about anything in the house, and he has put everything that he has in my charge. 9 He is not greater in this house than I am, nor has he kept back anything from me except yourself, because you are his wife. How then can I do this great wickedness and sin against God?

Notice how Joseph does not think about himself or of his own passions or desires. Instead, Joseph begins by first thinking about how his actions would affect Potiphar his master. One can speculate with certainty that Potiphar was not a perfect master. Yet, Joseph focused on the good things about his relationship with him. This then is the first step in which we are to take. We must not think of our own desires, but we must think of how our sin will affect others. So, those who are married should think of how their sin would affect their spouse and even their children.

Returning to the passage, one can also see that Joseph loved the Lord with all his heart for he could not bear the thought of how the act of adultery would affect his relationship with him. It was his love for God then which gave him the inner strength to turn his thoughts away from her and to him. This is therefore the second step. We must love God supremely. And in Matthew 22:37, this is what Jesus told the lawyer who asked him what the greatest commandment was, **And he said to him, "You shall love the Lord your God with all our heart and with all your soul and with all your mind."**

Then the third and final step can be seen in Genesis 39:11-12, **But one day, when he went into the house to do his work and none of the men of the house was there in the house, 12 she caught him by his garment, saying, "Lie with me." But he left his garment in her hand and fled and got out of the house.** Notice how Joseph fled. Since Joseph was able to keep his heart free from lust, he was then able to do the right thing in the moment of temptation. We must therefore follow his example and remove ourselves from anything which tempts us.

With this in mind, one will read in Matthew 5:29-30 where Jesus said:

29 If your right eye causes you to sin, tear it out and throw it away. For it is better that you lose one of your members than that your whole body be thrown into hell. 30 And if your right hand causes you to sin, cut it off and throw it away. For it is better that you lose one of your members than that your whole body go into hell."

Jesus taught that if one's right eye or right hand was causing them to sin, then it would be better for the individual to remove them. This may seem extreme to some, but if one actually believed there was eternal life or death awaiting them after this life, then they would be willing to do whatever it took to avoid eternal death (which is eternal punishment). So, the point Jesus was making is that lust or sexual immorality should be avoided at all costs. Therefore, if one finds themselves being tempted by internet pornography, then it would be better for them to throw their computer away. If one should find themselves being tempted by movies or television shows, then it would be better for them to throw their television away than to suffer eternal punishment.

Now the next threat to be discussed is falsehood. Because of one's sinful nature, one is inclined to bend the truth in order to have what they desire. In Matthew 5:33, Jesus addressed falsehood when he spoke of one making oaths and said, **"Again you have heard that it was said to those of old, 'You shall not swear falsely, but shall perform to the Lord what you have sworn.'** Jesus' statement was the combination of two laws. The words **'You shall not swear falsely...** was referring to Leviticus 19:12 which was a law forbidding individuals from swearing by God's name falsely. So, if one swore by God's name that what they said was of the truth, and it was not, then they would have profaned the name of God. Or if one swore by God's name that something would be done, and they failed to do it, then they would have also profaned the name of God. Now regarding the second law, the words **but shall perform to the Lord what you have sworn'** was referring to Deuteronomy 23:21. This was a law regarding individuals who made an oath to God. So, if their vow to God was not fulfilled, then the person would have become guilty of sin. By combining these two laws, Jesus was simply telling the people that what he was about to say related to all oaths.

With this in mind, Jesus then said in Matthew 5:34-37:

³⁴ But I say to you, Do not take an oath at all, either by heaven, for it is the throne of God, ³⁵ or by the earth, for it is his footstool, or by Jerusalem, for it is the city of the great King. ³⁶ And do not take an oath by your head, for you cannot make one hair white or black. ³⁷ Let what you say be simply 'Yes' or 'No'; anything more than this comes from evil."

At first glance, one would be inclined to think that Jesus was speaking against the Law, but this would not be true. When one looks closely at the Deuteronomy passage, they would see that oaths were made optional in the following verse, for one will read in 23:22, **But if you refrain from vowing, you will not be guilty of sin**. Therefore, when the people heard this, they would have known that Jesus was simply upholding the Law as he encouraged his followers and others to refrain from making oaths. Jesus then solidified his position further by revealing that everything inevitably belonged to God. To swear by the heavens was to swear by God for they were his throne. To swear by the earth was to swear by God for it was his footstool. To swear by Jerusalem, the city of the great King, was to swear by God for it was his city, and it was he who appointed the great King. Even to swear by one's own head was to swear by God for he was their Creator. So then, to not fulfill *any* oath was in actuality a sin against God. So, the point Jesus was making was this; one should value truth and despise falsehood at all times, for when one did, they would then not need to make an oath to validate what they said was true. Jesus then encouraged his followers to do this and to simply use "yes" or "no," for anything else came from evil.

But one may wonder just how dangerous falsehood can really be, for after all a little white lie here and there is nothing like murder or adultery. But one should keep in mind Jesus' warning when he said in Matthew 12:36, **I tell you, on the day of judgment people will give account for every careless word they speak.** Jesus' warning reveals the depth and intensity of God's judgment, for we will all one day have to give account to God for *every* false or evil thing we say. This is not only shocking but also frightful to think about. But this is not all, for if one accepts falsehood as being acceptable, and it is then accompanied by a desire, it could lead one down several unfavorable directions. For instance, the road of falsehood could lead one in the direction of deceit (Romans 1:29; 1 Peter 2:1), for when one desires worldly power, they will bend the truth in order to manipulate others for their selfish gain. Or if falsehood is mixed with anger, it could lead one in the direction of slandering others in order to destroy reputations (Romans 1:30; Ephesians 4:31; Colossians 3:8; 1 Peter 2:1). And if falsehood is mixed with covetousness, it could lead one in the direction of becoming a swindler (1 Corinthians 5:11). So as one can see, falsehood is extremely dangerous and should not be taken lightly. It too should be avoided at all costs.

In this chapter, it was shown what love is, and that in order to abide in love, one must become pure in heart. One must cleanse their heart of evil emotions such as bitterness (which leads to hate), lust (which leads to sexual immorality), and to deny falsehood (for it leads to such things as deceitfulness, slandering or to swindling). Yet, these are just three of the five destructive sins of the heart, for Jesus also warned his followers of the sin of covetousness, which will be covered in chapter six, and of pride, which will be covered in chapter seven. It is these five sins of the heart in which the child of God must learn to avoid.

Summary Questions

1. What is the biblical meaning of love?

2. To abide in love means for one to have and to maintain a heart that is _____, free from evil emotions.

3. If one's anger is not kept in check, then it will eventually lead to bitterness, and then to what?

4. It is the act of _____ others which condemns one to hell, and anything which comes out of _____ is equal to murder for murder is merely the greatest expression of hate.

5. How does one remove anger from one's heart?
    a. R_____ who we are
    b. F_____ them
    c. P_____ for them

6. Having a _____ spirit thus becomes another sign of one who has the Spirit within them.

7. When dealing with evil people we must remember this; we are not at war with the people, we are at war with the evil within them. They are just a what?

8. If one's physical attraction towards another is not kept in check, then it will eventually lead to lust, and then to what?

9. How does one remove lust from one's heart?
    a. First, consider how your actions will affect _____.
    b. Then, think how your actions will affect your relationship with _____.
    c. Then, you should remove yourself from the _____.

10. If one comes to consider falsehood as being acceptable, what roads could they find themselves traveling upon?

11. Since our thoughts affect our emotions, by forcing ourselves to think a certain way; we can actually change how we are feeling. We can actually control your emotions. This is how you can abide in _____.

Notes

5
The Merciful Peacemaker

In the previous chapters of this book, we learned that the divine nature of the only living God is love, and that the Spirit of God is also the Spirit of truth, so if one believes or confesses that they have received the Holy Spirit of God, then they will abide in both love and truth. This is therefore true repentance, and these are the signs of one having truly received salvation. But in order for one to abide in both love and truth, one must learn to keep their heart free from bitterness, lust, and falsehood. One could say that these were inner threats which will hinder the children of God from achieving their goal. But unfortunately, this is only half the battle for the children of God must also learn how to walk in love while living in this dark sinful world. Thus, the children of God must learn how to walk in love towards those who are godless (or atheists). They must learn how to properly relate to those who are evil (or those who live by the wicked ways of the world). Now with these things in mind, we will turn to the second characteristic in which Jesus used to describe those who are truly the children of God.

The Spirit of the Child of God

In Matthew 5:7 Jesus described the spirit of the children of God when he said, **Blessed are the merciful, for they shall receive mercy.** Notice how Jesus said it is the merciful who will receive God's mercy. This is to say that on the day of judgment, God will be merciful towards those who have shown others mercy. James echoes this same warning in his letter when he wrote, **For judgment is without mercy to one who has shown no mercy. Mercy triumphs over judgment** (James 2:13). But what does it mean for one to be merciful to others? One may answer quickly by saying it simply means that the child of God is to forgive those who have wronged them or who have offended them. And this answer would be correct, for once again in Matthew 6:14-15 Jesus said, **For if you forgive others their trespasses, your heavenly Father will also forgive you. ¹⁵ but if you do not forgive others their trespasses, neither will your Father forgive your trespasses.** So, the merciful are those who have been wronged by another, and though they have the right to demand justice, they choose instead to forgive.

However, there is another aspect of mercy in which many individuals do not consider. With this in mind, I would like to point out a pattern that is seen with the Matthew 5:7 and 6:14-15 passages. The pattern is this: what we do to others is what God will do to us on the day of judgment. So, if we are merciful to others, God will be merciful to us, and if we are forgiving of others, God will be forgiving of us. Now there is another trait with this exact same pattern within Jesus' sermon, and it is found in Matthew 7:1. In this passage Jesus says **"Judge not, that you be not judged.** Since scripture clearly teaches that everyone will stand before the judgment seat of

God (See Romans 14:10; 2 Corinthians 5:10), Jesus was therefore referring to each individual act of judgment that one makes. In other words, each time one judge's others, they will have to give account of it to God. This is supported by the Matthew 12:36 passage in which we saw how one will be judged by God for every careless word they say. With this in mind, it is therefore wise for one to avoid judging others, for in the following verse one will read, **For with the judgment you pronounce you will be judged, and with the measure you use it will be measured to you.** Now since it is only these two traits which have this pattern, it is in this way then that Jesus has defined for his followers how they are to express mercy. They are to be forgiving and nonjudgmental of others. But please keep in mind that there is a distinction between judging others and correcting others. Judging others comes with sentencing while the correcting of others does not. In fact, according to 2 Timothy 3:16, it is encouraged to correct others by the word of God, as long as it is done in love.

    Yet, there are times when one must judge others. This is seen in the church discipline passages and in passages regarding those who had tried to turn the churches towards accepting a false gospel (1 Corinthians 5:11-13 & Galatians 1:6-9). What then? The next verse sheds light on this for Jesus said, **Why do you see the speck that is in your brother's eye, but do not notice the log that is in your own eye?** Though Jesus was emphasizing why one should not judge others, his words also reveal an important principle. When one does have to judge another, one should do so in a unhypocritical way. In other words, one should judge others with the knowledge that they too are with sin (Galatians 6:1).

    On a personal note, in my effort to not judge others, I have learned that I tend to judge others quickly without really thinking. It is like an uncontrollable reflex. Frustrated by this, upon further reflection, it would seem I also have the uncanny ability to forget my own offences. And once they are forgotten, I then will develop a false impression of myself, one in which I have done nothing wrong. One could say I wear this false impression of myself as a mask, and this then leads to pride entering my heart. So, with a false impression of myself and because of pride, I will then judge others instantly, without fear in that I am equally as guilty before God. However, from the judgmental statements I hear from others, it would seem that I am not the only one with this problem.

Yet the solution to this is simple, we must take off our masks. So, instead of forgetting our past sins, *we must remember them.* We must therefore add this practice to our prayer time, and by doing so, we will then reside within a humbled state. And from this humbled state, we will then respond appropriately, for we will be well aware of our own sinfulness. I believe this to be the reason why the Apostle John mentions that we should confess our sins to God, for in 1 John 1:8-9 he wrote, **If we say we have no sin, we deceive ourselves, and the truth is not in us. ⁹ If we confess our sins, he is faithful and just to forgive us our sins and to cleanse us from all unrighteousness.** This practice is not to reveal our sin to God, for he is already well aware of them, but it is to keep us humble and free from pride.

To now summarize what has been covered up to this point, in order to abide in love, we must purge our hearts of any bitterness, lust, falsehood, covetousness, and pride. Then, in order to walk in love towards others, we must possess a merciful spirit, which is to be forgiving and nonjudgmental of others. It is only then, when we possess a pure heart and the right spirit, that we will be able to truly treat others the way we would like to be treated. It is only then when we will be able to abide and walk in love and truth.

What Does Walking in Love and Truth Look Like?

Now when one walks in love and truth towards others, it is then when one will become a peacemaker. In Matthew 5:9 Jesus said, **Blessed are the peacemakers, for they shall be called sons of God.** The term "peacemaker" merely describes how the children of God will relate to those who are evil and how they will react to their wicked words and actions. But once again please keep in mind, to refer to one as being evil is simply another way of describing one who is simply living by the ways of the world.

So, with this in mind, when Jesus began to describe the appropriate responses of the children of God, he began by first quoting the law. In Matthew 5:38 Jesus said, **"You have heard that it was said, 'An eye for an eye and a tooth for a tooth'** (Exodus 21:24). This was simply a way of saying that the one who suffered loss or harm was justified in seeking retribution. They had the right to harm their offender in the same way in which they were harmed. They had the right to take from their offender what was taken from them. Though this was appropriate for the judges, it was not for the child of God, for Jesus then said in verse 39, **But I say to you, Do not resist the one who is evil.** Now this is the first of two statements which will serve to define what it means to be a peacemaker. But his first statement reveals that the children of God, the merciful peacemakers, were not to seek justice. They were not to resist the one who was evil. So, in order to clarify his statement, Jesus then gave four examples.

The first example is stated in the second half of verse 39, **But if anyone slaps you on the right cheek, turn to him the other also.** In this illustration, the child of God has done nothing wrong, and yet they are being physically assaulted by another. Nevertheless, Jesus instructed his followers to not resist. In fact, if their offender wished to strike them again, they were to let them by offering the other cheek. God's people are simply not to retaliate or defend themselves against the one who is evil. Does this seem crazy? It should for it is not the way of the world. It is the way of God.

Now the next example is found in verse 40, **And if anyone would sue you and take your tunic, let him have your cloak as well.** In this situation, the child of God, who again has done nothing wrong, is being assaulted financially. And once again Jesus taught that the child of God was not to resist the one who is evil, but when being sued, they were to not only let them have what they were suing them for, but they were to also give them extra! Does this also sound insane? If it does, it is because we are accustomed to living according to the ways of the world. But now that we are one of God's children, we must learn to set aside our worldly ways. We must come to accept our heavenly Father's way and learn to walk this difficult path of love.

With this being said, we must become properly motivated in order to make this difficult journey. But what do I mean by this? If one is not properly motivated, they will fall by the wayside. They will abandon this path for it is an exceedingly challenging path to travel. So, in order to make this journey through life, we must come to love God *more* than the world. And when this happens, we will then have the motivation we need to break free from all forms of covetousness. We will then have the ability to let go of temporary things, such as our money or possessions, in order express love towards others. This will be discussed in greater detail in the following chapter.

Now turning to the third example in Matthew 5:41, **And if anyone forces you to go one mile, go with him two miles.** Once again, the child of God is innocent for they have done nothing wrong. Yet in this example they are being attacked, and this time it is regarding their labor. Notice that instead of the child of God being asked, they are being forced to go a mile by the authority which is over them. So, even though the child of God is being treated harshly and unfairly by the authority over them, Jesus taught that they were to not only go the mile, which was asked of them, but they were to also go with them an additional mile.

Then in Matthew 5:42, one will read of Jesus' fourth example in which he says, **Give to the one who begs from you, and do not refuse the one who would borrow from you."** At first glance, one may think that Jesus was simply telling his followers to give to those in need. Yet this is not the case, for once again the context of these four examples is on how the peacekeeper is to not resist the one who is evil. Therefore, the child of God is to give to the one who begs from them, even if the individual does not have a legitimate need. In other words, they are to give to the individual even if they know it is a scam!

To support this, Jesus then said in Luke 6:34-36:

[34] And if you lend to those from whom you expect to receive, what credit is that to you? Even sinners lend to sinners, to get back the same amount. [35] But love your enemies, and do good, and lend, expecting nothing in return, and your reward will be great, and you will be sons

of the Most High, for he is kind to the ungrateful and the evil. **36 Be merciful, even as your Father is merciful.**

Jesus' words are quite clear. We are to love our enemies, we are to do good things for them, and we are to lend to them expecting nothing in return. Once again, in order to do this, money and possessions must have little value to the child of God.

You are maybe wondering now how one could live this way and still provide for their family, but you must understand that Jesus was making a point. He was revealing to the people the way of God and how sharply it conflicted with the ways of the world. He was showing that when one became a merciful peacemaker, people will become of more value to the child of God than their money or possessions.

With this being said, giving to others should be done wisely. Though Jesus lived by these principles and gave to those who were in need, he also ensured the needs of his disciples were also met. A simple way to look at this is that one does not sacrifice people in order to help other people, for this is not the way of love. In 1 Timothy 5:8 one will read, **But if anyone does not provide for his relatives, and especially for members of his household, he has denied the faith and is worse than an unbeliever.** So, when one gives to others, one does so but not to the expense of their own family members. If one does, then they have become worse than an unbeliever. Also, one does not give to the point in which they become a burden to the church. One will read in 1 Timothy 8:16, **If any believing woman has relatives who are widows, let her care for them. Let the church not be burdened, so that it may care for those who are truly widows.** Since the church's resources are limited, one must do their best to meet their own needs. This is to ensure that the resources of the church go to those who are truly in need. So, as one can see, one is to give to the one who is evil, but one should do so wisely.

Along this same line of thought, there is something which must be addressed, and that is debt. Though I have no desire to get into the topic of money management, for I am no expert, one must have the means to express love. One must have the means to help others. With this being said, one must come to see debt for what it truly is, an enemy. It is something which robs one of opportunities to help others. One must therefore, remove as much of their debt as possible. And in order to do this, one must learn to live below their means. One must break free from their worldly desires and stop spending all their wealth upon themselves. Then by doing so, one will have the means to pay off their debt, build a savings account for emergencies, and to help others.

Turning now to Jesus' second statement, which also defines a peacemaker, he said in Matthew 5:43-44, **You have heard that it was said, 'You shall love your neighbor and hate your enemy.' **44** But I say to you, love your enemies and pray for those who persecute you…** Thou this passage was used in chapter four to reveal the process of forgiving others, it also reveals how the peacemaker will not only not resist the one who is evil, but they will also walk in love towards their enemies. Knowing how this would seem unrealistic to his audience, Jesus then explained that as a child of God their behavior would become like that of their heavenly Father's. Since God is a loving God, who cares for both the good and the evil and meets their needs, which is seen by the sun rising on both and the rain being sent to both, the child of God will do likewise. They will seek to care for the needs of both the good and the evil. So, in order to enter God's kingdom, one must become perfect as their heavenly Father is perfect (Matthew 5:20 & 48). One must walk in love towards *all* individuals.

Being Led by the Spirit

In Romans 8:14, Paul revealed an interesting concept when he wrote, **For all who are led by the Spirit of God are sons of God.** But what does it mean to be led by the Spirit of God? According to context it would seem Paul was speaking of our desires, for in the previous verse he wrote, **For if you live according to the flesh** (which is to live according to one's worldly desires) **you will die, but if by the Spirit you put to death the deeds of the body, you will live.** (v. 13) Since the divine nature of God is love, and because God's love is poured into our heats by his Spirit (Romans 5:5), and because we are led through life by what we desire, to be led by the Spirit then is to be led by our love for God and others. Now consider this for a moment, is it not true that when we help others, we come to enjoy the feeling we receive? Do we not come to enjoy seeing the joy and appreciation on the faces of those in whom we have helped? If so, then could we not begin to appreciate this and desire to have this experience more and more in our life? Therefore, instead of being led through life by our covetousness desires, we could become led through life by our love for God and the desire to minister to those around us.

Yet there is more to being led by the Spirit of God for there is much more to his Spirit than just love. For instance, the Spirit is also a Spirit of power, for it is he who enables us to overcome the spirit of sin within us and the evil one, and it is he who enables us to carry out the Father's will by supplying us with the abilities or skillset needed. Then also, the Spirit is a Spirit of wisdom and of revelation (Ephesians 1:18-19) for it is he who imparts to us the wisdom of God so we can make the right decisions in life, and it is he who speaks to us revealing hidden truths found in God's word. So, as you can see, the Spirit is not just love and he is not just a power source, he is a person (See Ephesians 4:30). The Spirit of God is our Helper, Teacher, Guide, and Counselor. Thus, to be led by the Spirit is much more than to just be led by the desire to love others, it is to be led by the divine presence of our God.

But what we will soon discover is that the spirit of sin, which is within us, will still have the ability to oppose our efforts even though we now have the Holy Spirit. And since our minds can control our emotions (or desires) which in turn guide us through life, the two will both seek to influence our minds. Our minds will therefore become conflicted. One set of memories, thoughts, and ideas will bring about good emotions within us and enable us to carry out the will of God while the other one will not. This is why I refer to "sin," as Paul described in Romans 7:11, as the spirit of sin for it has the ability to manipulate and to deceive us, thus having intelligence. Whereas to say "our sinful nature" simply denotes a reflexive action in which one does naturally without thinking.

Now with this in mind, what we will soon discover is that one set of memories will produce within us a godly grief as we are reminded of our past mistakes. But godly grief will not produce death but instead will bring us to repentance (2 Corinthians 7:9-10). Also, these memories will keep us in a humbled state, which we now know is necessary in order for us to walk in truth and love. And not only will thoughts enter our minds making connections between verses in which hidden truths within God's word are revealed, but ideas will also enter our minds on ways in which we could improve our walk and to help others. And since such things as these will produce peace, joy, thankfulness, assurance, and hope within us, we will know they are of the Holy Spirit.

But then there are the other set of memories, thoughts, and ideas, which will hinder us or lead us away from doing the will of God. Memories will pop into our minds of those who have hurt us in the past, thus causing hate and resentment to rise up within our hearts all over again. This is death. Then, there are individuals in the present who are tormenting or irritating us. Because of their actions, we may begin to imagine bad things happening to them. And then there are thoughts about having certain possessions that we want, not need, that will bombard our minds. Also, because of our desire to be liked by others, ideas will pop into our minds of sarcastic jokes or things we could say or do to others which would be funny. But when examined closely, we will see that these jokes would be inappropriate of a child of God, and they would hurt the feelings of those we joke with or about. Such memories, thoughts, and ideas as these will be of the spirit of sin within us, for they will produce pain and sorrow and will generate within us anger, confusion, frustration, doubt, and worry.

Now with these things in mind, in order to be led by the Spirit of God, we must learn how to be sensitive to this and to recognize who is influencing us, and this is done by examining our thoughts and choosing which ones we will allow ourselves to think about. The Apostle Paul wrote in Philippians 4:8, **Finally, brothers, whatever is true, whatever is honorable, whatever is just, whatever is pure, whatever is lovely, whatever is commendable, if there is any excellence, if there is anything worthy of praise, think about these things.** We must learn then how to *set* our minds on the Spirit

(Romans 8 & Colossians 3:2). If our thoughts are true, honorable, just, pure, lovely, and commendable, then they are of the Holy Spirit. We can continue to think on them and allow them to influence us and direct us. If they are not, then we must immediately stop ourselves from dwelling on them and return our thoughts to the things of God.

Also, there are several practices we can do that will aid us in keeping our minds set on the Spirit. They are to pray continuously, sing spiritual songs, and to meditate on God's word (1 Thessalonians 5:17; Ephesians 5:18-20; & Colossians 3:16). Though these may seem petty and awkward at first, there is a reason why the apostles suggested these to their followers. It is because these practices work. They will make a major difference in your walk with the Lord. But as you can see, to abide and to walk in love, and to be led by the Spirit, will change your life significantly. You will become sanctified unto God.

The Path Less Traveled

However, even though this is an amazing life, not many people will choose to travel this path, simply because the Way is an extremely difficult path to travel. It is a path in which God's people will be taken advantage of, abused, and even persecuted. It is a path of suffering. And it is for this reason that the last two beatitudes refer to persecution. In Matthew 5:10-12 one will read:

[10] Blessed are those who are persecuted for righteousness sake, for theirs is the kingdom of heaven. [11] Blessed are you when others revile you and persecute you and utter all kinds of evil against you falsely on my account. [12] Rejoice

and be glad, for your reward is great in heaven, for so they persecuted the prophets who were before you.

But even with Christ's promise of heavenly rewards, most will reject the Way simple because they cannot live this way. But I would like to remind you of Jesus' words in Matthew 7:13-14, **Enter by the narrow gate. For the gate is wide and the way is easy that leads to destruction, and those who enter by it are many. ¹⁴ For the gate is narrow and the way is hard that leads to life, and those who find it are few."** This is clearly a warning, but in order to comprehend the warning one must first come to realize that one cannot separate the narrow gate from the Way. So, with this in mind, those who choose to enter the narrow gate of faith in Jesus Christ and to walk his Way, though it is difficult, will find eternal life, for that is where the gate and the difficult path will lead. However, those who claim to have entered through the narrow gate of faith, though they travel the easy path, will only find destruction, for that is simply where the easy path will lead. So now the question is this, "Which path will you choose?"

Summary Questions

1. What does it mean for one to be merciful to others?

2. What is the difference between judging others or correcting others?

3. In order to keep ourselves from judging others instantly, instead of _____ our past sins, we must _____ them.

4. There are times when we must judge others, so how are we to do this?

5. Being a peacemaker, means we are not to _____ those who are evil.
   a. When physically assaulted we are not to retaliate or defend ourselves.
   b. When being sued, we are to not only let them have what they were suing us for, but we are to also give them extra.
   c. When treated harshly by the authority over us, we are to not only go the mile they ask of us, but to also give them an additional mile.
   d. When asked, we are to give to others even if they will not repay you or return your things.

6. To do this, money and possessions must have little _____, and one must love God _____.

7. As a peacemaker, Jesus said we are to _____ our enemies and _____ for those who persecute us. Thus, we will be merciful and kind, doing good deeds towards them.

8. What does it mean to be led by the Spirit of God?

9. In order to be led by the Spirit, we must set our minds upon him. How does one do this?

Notes

6
The Overcomers

If you now have the desire to repent, by following the Way of Jesus Christ, then you need to be aware of the two greatest threats in which you will face on your journey. These two threats have lured many individuals away from the path of love and truth, for they target our motivation. And if you recall, our motivation is the thing which drives us and keeps us going. With this in mind, Jesus taught that the greatest commandment in the Law was to love God supremely, and the reason for this is that it is impossible for us to repent and to walk in love unless we do, for the love we have for our heavenly Father is the very reason why we choose to live this way. It is the reason why we keep getting up after we have been knocked down by sin. With this being said, these two threats are not fierce or frightful but are instead beautiful and appealing. Yet, because of their mesmerizing qualities, it is not until the very end when one will fully realize their true destructive powers. So, the purpose of this chapter is to make you aware of these two threats so you can overcome them, and they are both found in the Parable of the Sower.

The Two Greatest Threats

The Parable of the Sower is found in three of the four gospels which are Matthew, Mark, and Luke. Now when one examines the three accounts, they will see that there are slight differences between them. These variances are not errors but simply represent what people genuinely heard and remembered while under the influence of the Holy Spirit. Also, one should consider this as well; this parable, along with the others, were taught by Jesus more than once as he went from town to town, and it would be foolish to think that Jesus did not also tailor them to the people in which he spoke too (See Matthew 13:34; Mark 4:1). So, with this in mind, when all three accounts are placed together, these variations become a benefit to us for it is then when one will obtain a deeper and broader understanding of the parable in which Jesus taught. Now let us begin by reading Luke 8:4-8:

⁴ And when a great crowd was gathering and people from town after town came to him, he said in a parable: ⁵ "A sower went out to sow his seed. And as he sowed, some fell along the path and was trampled underfoot, and the birds of the air devoured it. ⁶ And some fell on the rock, and as it grew up, it withered away, because it had no moisture. ⁷ And some fell among thorns, and the thorns grew up with it and choked it. ⁸ And some fell into good soil and grew and yielded a hundredfold." As he said these things, he called out, "He who has ears to hear, let him hear."

At first Jesus' disciples did not understand the parable, but when they were alone with him, they then asked him what it meant (v. 9). Jesus began by first explaining to them that the seed represented the word of God (v.11). Even though the "word of God" would entail everything we refer to as the Old Testament, or the entire Jewish Scriptures, much more was implied. For instance, the "word of God" would include Jesus' interpretation of the Scriptures and also his additional teachings on such things as how one could enter the kingdom of God, for it was these in which Jesus referred to as the words of the heavenly Father (John 7:16; 14:24; 17:8). Also, one must not forget to include the three great commandments in which Jesus emphasized, for one was to believe in him as the Christ, love God supremely, and to love others as he had loved them (John 14:21-23; 1 John 2:4-7). So, with these additional things in mind, "the word of God" became something which could be accepted or rejected by the Jews and eventually the Gentiles. Hence, the "word" causes division.

The Seed Sown Along the Path

The first division is made between those who believe the "word of God" and those who do not. Jesus said in Luke 8:12, **The ones along the path are those who have heard; then the devil comes and takes away the word from their hearts, so that they may not believe and be saved.** According to Matthew 13:19, these are the ones who will hear the word but who will not understand it. So, when viewing the two passages together, this group represents those who hear the word, and though they may not at first understand it, if given the time, they could come to comprehend it, believe it, and even become saved! But unfortunately, they are denied this opportunity, for before they can do this, Satan comes along and takes the seed from their heart. This could be either through distraction, deception, or both.

Jesus then began to describe the next group, which represents those who hear and believe the word. However, not all who believe the word will enter the kingdom of God. As the word is sown in the hearts of the people, there will be three types of believers which will develop.

The Seed Sown on Rocky Ground

The first type of believer was said to have been sown on rocky ground. In Luke 8:13 one will read, **And the ones on the rock are those who, when they hear the word, receive it with joy. But these have no root; they believe for a while, and in time of testing fall away.** Emphasis should be placed on the fact that these individuals heard and believed the gospel. The passage even says that they **received it with joy** which would imply that they had placed their faith in Jesus Christ for salvation. But even though they had done these things, it was also said they had no root, for there were simply too many rocks within the soil of their heart. So, in other words, because of these rocks, they were basically unable to grow substantial roots in order to receive the moisture needed to flourish. Thus, when the heat of persecution came, they dried up and fell away. These individuals will be referred to as shallow believers.

But what do the rocks or stones represent? They represent a love of self. This love of self is therefore the first threat in which the child of God must overcome. Now what does the moisture represent? The moisture represents their love for God. So, even though these individuals believed and trusted in Jesus Christ as their Lord and Savior and even had a love of

God within them, God was not their dominant love. It was themselves instead. They simply loved themselves more than they loved God. Hence, they had no moisture. Then, when persecution came along, they fell away by denying Jesus. In Matthew 10:32-33, Jesus told his disciples, **"So everyone who acknowledges me before men, I also will acknowledge before my Father who is in heaven, but whoever denies me before men, I also will deny before my Father who is in heaven.** However, as one can see by Peter's example, one mistake does not mean the end, for one can change and begin to love Jesus Christ supremely. Nonetheless, in order to truly make the sacrifices needed in order to follow Jesus, one must love him more than one's own life (Luke 9:23-24).

The denial of Jesus can come in many forms and at many different levels. For example, when one wants to be accepted by others, the shallow believer will go along with what is being said, even if those in whom they seek to impress are speaking negatively of the Lord. Because of their fear of being mocked and rejected, they will remain silent and will not take a stand for Jesus. Their desire to be accepted by others is simply greater than their love for the Lord. Also, the shallow believer will be reluctant to reveal to others they are Christian, especially if it will negatively affect their carriers or image. If asked, these individuals will deny him for they will love their career or image more than him. To simply put it, the shallow believer will always put themselves first. This is once again due to their dominant love being themselves instead of God. And finally, one's love for oneself is what ultimately keeps many individuals from accepting the Way. They simply cannot set aside their ambition and become a servant to all, or they cannot live in a way which would allow them to be taken advantage of or abused by others. Though these individuals believe they are saved, Jesus taught that those who lived this way would not receive eternal life. They will therefore be denied as they denied him.

The Seed Sown Among Thorns

In Luke 8:14, Jesus then described the next group of believers, **And as for what fell among the thorns, they are those who hear, but as they go on their way they are choked by the cares and riches and pleasures of life, and their fruit does not mature.** These are also individuals who have heard the word, believed the gospel, and placed their faith in Jesus Christ trusting in him for their salvation. But unfortunately, as with the previous group, they too had hearts of poor soil, and even though they began to produce, their fruit was unable to mature. Now the reason why their fruit did not mature was because even though they believed and started to follow the Way, they also had weeds within the soil of their heart. These weeds represent worldly desires. So, instead of pursuing the kingdom of God, they began to pursue worldly riches and pleasures. Then over time their faith became choked by the weeds. These individuals represent worldly believers who simply began to love the world more than God, and this is the second threat in which the child of God must overcome.

Now this threat of worldliness affects everyone, both rich and poor, for even the one who is poor can become consumed with obtaining wealth and possessions. Thus, worldliness is not about how much one owns; it is about the state of one's heart. So, in order to illustrate worldliness and how it can hinder one from becoming fruitful, I would like to present the following thought process in which many worldly believers tend to follow. It begins like this: Whenever a worldly believer sees a need, they will look away. They will tell themselves they have nothing to give for they too are struggling. However, the reason they are struggling and believe they have nothing to give is because they have already spent their wealth upon themselves. They have overextended themselves in order to live the best life they can with what they had. So, as a result of this, they will go through life believing they have had nothing to give towards helping others, and yet, they have had plenty. The Apostle John says in 1 John 2:15-16, **Do not love the world or the things in the world. If anyone loves the world, the love of the Father is not in him. 16 For all that is in the world-the desires of the flesh and the desires of the eyes and pride of life-is not from the Father but is from the world.**

With this in mind, each and every believer is faced with a choice. They must choose to either live the best they can in this present life, which is to strive for wealth and possessions, or to live the best they can for the next life, which is to deny oneself in this life and live according to the Way. Jesus taught in Matthew 6:24, **No one can serve two masters, for either he will hate the one and love the other, or he will be devoted to the one and despise the other. You cannot serve God and money."**

But please keep in mind that what I have just written does not mean that if one chooses God then one cannot have wealth, possessions, or a successful career, for these things may well be found along one's path. However, it does mean that these things will not represent what the child of God with wealth is *pursuing*. Since God is their Master, their love for him will be far greater than their love for their wealth and possessions. Because of this, they will not only seek to live a life pleasing to God, but they will also focus on ways in which they can use their wealth to help others and to benefit the kingdom of God. This concept is seen in Luke 8:1-3, for when speaking of Jesus' ministry, Luke wrote:

¹ Soon afterward he went on through cities and villages, proclaiming and bringing the good news of the kingdom of God. And the twelve were with him, ² and also some women who had been healed of evil spirits and infirmities: Mary, called Magdalene, from whom seven demons had gone out, ³ and Joanna, the wife of Chuza, Herod's household manager, and Susanna, and many others, who provided for them out their means.

Notice how there were individuals who, out of their means, provided for the needs of both Jesus and his disciples. Unlike the wealthy young man, Jesus did not request for them to give up everything they owned to the poor and to follow him. This was simply because they did not covet their wealth as the young man, which can easily be seen by their willingness to financially support Jesus' ministry. And because God meant more to them than their wealth, these individuals were able to then serve an important role, for they made it possible for Jesus to travel from town-to-town healing and proclaiming the good news. So, as one can see, there is a great need for those who have been blessed by God with wealth, but who are also solely focused on the kingdom of heaven. Thus, rich or poor, God must become one's dominant love. One must come to love God supremely over everything else.

Unfortunately, as with the previous threat, the threat of worldliness will lead many astray. Though there will be many who will believe and trust in Jesus Christ for their salvation, they will refuse to follow the Way. They will refuse to live below their means. They will refuse to live in a way which will allow them to help others. They will do this for they will simply love the world more than they love God.

The Seed Sown on Good Soil

In Luke 8:15, Jesus then described the last group of believers, **As for that in the good soil, they are those who, hearing the word, hold it fast in an honest and good heart, and bear fruit with patience."** These individuals represent the *true* children of God. According to the gospel of Matthew, what made the difference between these believers and the shallow and worldly believers is that they not only heard and believed the word of God, but they also understood it. In Matthew 13:23, **As for what was sown on good soil, this is the one who hears the word and understands it...** In other words, they understood the gospel in its entirety. They not only understood Jesus to be the Christ, the Son of God who died a sacrificial death for their sins and who rose from the grave, but they also understood the Way of Christ and comprehended its complete value. Then, according to the gospel of Mark, the true believers were those who accepted it. In Mark 4:20 one will read, **But those that were sown on the good soil are the ones who hear the word and accept it and bear fruit...** They not only accepted Jesus Christ as their Lord and Savior, but they also accepted his Way as their new way of life. Then, in the gospel of Luke, the true believers were those who upon hearing the word of God, held his precious word fast in an honest and good heart. In other words, since God became their dominant love, when faced with persecution or worldly desires, they would continue to hold him and his Way fast to the very end. So, when one puts all three gospel accounts together, it then becomes those who fully understand, accept, and hold fast the true gospel of Jesus Christ, which includes the Way, in an honest and good heart. It is they who will bear fruit in keeping with repentance, but they will do so with patience. Which is to say that their fruit is slowly maturing over time as they patiently wait for the return of their Lord and Savior Jesus Christ, as they patiently endure the hardships of living in this dark world, and as they patiently endure the trials of living righteously among the worldly.

Our Covetous Nature

So, how does one know if they are a shallow believer, a worldly believer, or a true believer? The answer to this question was given by Jesus in Matthew 6:19-21 when he said:

[19] Do not lay up for yourselves treasures on earth, where moth and rust destroy and where thieves break in and steal, [20] but lay up for yourselves treasures in heaven, where neither moth nor rust destroys and were thieves do not break in and steal. [21] For where your treasure is, there you heart will be also.

In this passage, Jesus urged his followers to collect heavenly treasures instead of earthly treasures. Why? Earthly treasures are temporary while heavenly treasures are eternal. Then in verse 21, Jesus pointed out that a person will acquire *what they value*. So, if one values the things of God, then that is what they will collect. If one values the things of the world, then that is what they will collect. Therefore, if one truly desires to know what it is that they genuinely love, then all they have to do is look at what they are collecting.

But what are heavenly treasures? The answer to this question is found in the twelfth chapter of Luke's gospel. Just after Jesus finished speaking to the crowd on the dangers of denying him and speaking against the Holy Spirit, a man called out to him from the crowd asking him to tell his brother to divide their inheritance. Apparently, the man's brother thought highly of Jesus, which then led him to believe that if Jesus told his brother to do this, then his brother would have done it. However, Jesus sternly replies that this was not his task to perform. Then seeing an opportunity to speak about the dangers of covetousness, for the two brothers were endangering their relationship with one another by fighting over possessions, one will read in verse 15, **And he said to them, "Take care, and be on your guard against all covetousness, for one's life does not consist in the abundance of his possessions."** Jesus pointed out how the man's actions were foolish for he was placing possessions before his brother, but the true essence of one's life consisted in the people around them. In other words, the people in one's life are far more important than one's possessions. With this in mind, and with what we learned in chapter three, the answer then is that our heavenly treasure are the people we lead to the Lord and the rewards we receive by doing loving deeds of mercy and kindness (Mark 9:41). And the act of coveting things simply becomes a distraction causing us to lose sight of what is important in this life.

Jesus then illustrated this principle with a parable. In Luke 12:16-21 one will read:

[16] And he told them a parable, saying, "The land of a rich man produced plentifully, [17] and he thought to himself,

'What shall I do, for I have nowhere to store my crops?" [18] And he said, 'I will do this: I will tear down my barns and build larger ones, and there I will store all my grain and my goods. [19] And I will say to my soul, Soul, you have ample goods laid up for many years; relax, eat, drink, be merry.' [20] But God said to him, 'Fool! This night your soul is required of you, and the things you have prepared, whose will they be?' [21] So is the one who lays up treasure for himself and is not rich toward God."

The wealthy landowner had been blessed with a bountiful harvest. But instead of sharing his wealth with the poor, he decided to build larger barns in order to store his extra grain. This revealed how he was more concerned about himself than for others. Because he coveted the idea of having a relaxing life in which he could eat, drink, and be merry, he missed the opportunity to help those who were suffering. Yet, God intervened and scolded the man for his foolishness for his time on earth was finished and now his wealth would fall into the hands of another. The point to the parable is that this man's covetousness robbed him of the opportunity to store up treasures in heaven. It distracted him from caring for the people in his life (See Cornelius in Acts 10).

So, in order for us to be able to focus on the needs of those around us, we must learn to avoid this sin of covetousness. We must not make the same mistake as the wealthy landowner, and we do this by setting our hearts on being content with what God has provided us. With this being said, a question which now comes to mind is this: with what then are we to be content? First, we are to be content with our salary. In Luke 3:14, one will read of several soldiers who asked John the Baptist this question, **"And we, what shall we do?" And he said** to them, "Do not extort money from anyone by threats or by false accusation, and be content with your wages." Then second, we are to be content with the money and possessions we have. One will read in Hebrews 13:5, **Keep your life free from love of money, and be content with what you have, for he has said, "I will never leave you nor forsake you."** Please take notice of the promise at the end of this verse for God says he will never leave nor forsake his people. In other words, God watches over his people closely and he will provide for their needs. We must therefore trust in God to sustain us and not worry about the future. Then lastly one will read in 1 Timothy 6:6-8:

6 Now there is great gain in godliness with contentment, 7 for we brought nothing into the world, and we cannot take anything out of the world. 8 But if we have food and clothing, with these we will be content.

So, the word of God clearly reveals that we are to be content with what God has given us. And when we are being pulled along in life by the desires of our heart for a better life, a better career, a bigger salary, a bigger and better home, a nicer and newer vehicle, we are in actuality following our covetous nature. Instead of being content with what God has given us, we are following the worldly desires of our heart. The Apostle Paul wrote in Romans 8:5-8:

5 For those who live according to the flesh set their minds on the things of the flesh, but those who live according to the Spirit set their minds on the things of the Spirit. 6 For to set the mind on the flesh is death, but to set the mind on the Spirit is life and peace. 7 For the mind that is set on

the flesh is hostile to God, for it does not submit to God's law; indeed, it cannot. **⁸ Those who are in the flesh cannot please God.**

So, to answer the question of what type of believer you are? Once again, look at what you are collecting. Look at what you seem to always be setting your mind upon. Look at the desires of your heart to see what is pulling you along in life. If you do not like what you see, then seek to change what you value. But most importantly, seek to love God supremely, for this must take place within your heart if you are going to ever truly repent.

Summary Questions

1. As a child of God, what led us to choose to live the Way of Christ and what motivates us to keep going?

2. In the Parable of the Sower, regarding the seed sown on rocky ground, emphasis should be placed on the fact that they did what?

3. But because of stones, the plants were unable to grow substantial roots, and when the heat of persecution came, they dried up and fell away. These individuals are referred to as _____ believers.

4. But what do the rocks or stones represent?

5. Regarding the seed sown among thorns, even though they began to produce, their fruit was unable to mature. So, what do the weeds represent?

6. Worldliness affects both rich and poor for it is the _____ of one's heart.

7. We are faced with a choice on how to live this life, so what is that choice?

8. Does this mean we cannot have wealth, possessions, or a successful career in this life?
If we can, then why?

9. What does the seed on good soil represent?

10. So, what are the two greatest threats to our motivation?

11. So how does one know if they are a shallow believer, a worldly believer, or a true believer?

12. What represents heavenly treasure and what will distract us from collecting them?

THE OVERCOMERS

Notes

7
The Prerequisite to Change

There once was a vase who thought it was a vessel of honor. Though it was not the most beautiful of vases, it was by far not the worst, at least in its opinion. But then one day, the Creator revealed to the vase the truth. The truth was that the vase was not a vessel of honor but of dishonor, for over the years it had become filled with trash. The vessel was heartbroken. Wanting to be a vessel of honor, the vase then tried to remove the trash within it by emptying itself out. Yet some trash still remained within the vase, and since the trash had been within the vase for a while, it had also left a dark stain. So, even though the vase was mostly empty of the trash, it still was unclean. The vase then cried out to the Creator for help. Since the Creator loved the vase, he began to do what was necessary in order to clean the vase. He began by first pouring hot water (the Holy Spirit) with soap (the Word) into the vase in order to remove the remaining trash. He then broke the vase into pieces, which enabled the Creator to then clean each piece meticulously with more soap and water until the stain from each piece was completely removed. He then rebuilt the vase by gluing the pieces back together. The vase is now a vessel of honor, for the Creator has declared it so, and the vase is now something in which the Creator can use. But the vase will never forget what the Lord had done for him, for every time he looks into the mirror, he sees the lines of where the pieces have been glued back together. And because of this experience, he has now become little Paul, a vessel in which God had to break in order to properly cleanse.

This is what must now happen in your life. You can remove most of the trash that is within your heart, but you cannot remove all of it. And you cannot remove the stain of pride, for only God can remove that stain. So, in order to remove the remaining trash and the stain, God will have to break you.

Death to the Old Self

The necessity of this event taking place in your life can be seen in Romans 6:3-4 in which the Apostle Paul wrote, **Do you not know that all of us who have been baptized into Christ Jesus were baptized into his death? ⁴ We were buried therefore with him by baptism into death, in order that, just as Christ was raised from the dead by the glory of the Father, we too might walk in newness of life.** In this passage, Paul connected the Lord's death to the practice of baptism and revealed how baptism by water illustrates a very important principle. First, when the new believer becomes completely submerged under water, they are seen as uniting with Jesus in the tomb. In other words, they have entered into his death. Then when the new believer is raised up out of the water, they are seen as uniting with Jesus as he rose from the grave. Just as Jesus was raised to newness of life, so then is the believer raised to walk in newness of life. Hence, there ought to be a change in the life of the individual.

So, how does this change happen? With this question in mind, Paul then wrote the following verses **⁶ We know that our old self was crucified with him in order that the body of sin might be brought to nothing, so that we would no longer be enslaved to sin. ⁷ For one who has died has been set free from sin.** Notice how the one who has died with Christ has been set free from their old body of sin. This is to say that their new self is no longer *enslaved* to the spirit of sin within them. The power of the spirit of sin, which once ruled their body, has been brought to nothing, or in other words, it has been neutralized by the Holy Spirit. So, according to Paul, in order for one to change one must become crucified with Christ. The old self must die on the cross with Jesus, for it is only then when one will truly become free from the controlling influence of the spirit of sin within them and become a new creation. Only then will one be able to walk in newness of life.

The Process of Dying

Returning again to Jesus' sermon on the Mount in Matthew's gospel, Jesus began his sermon by giving a list of nine characteristics which describe the children of God, five of which have already been covered. These characteristics are known as the "beatitudes." At first glance they will seem to be speaking of the poor and lowly. And this was true, to some extent, for in Luke's version Jesus specifically blessed the poor and then pronounced woes over the wealthy. This was largely due to the wealthy, as seen by Jesus' two parables of the Wealthy Landowner and the Rich Man and Lazarus, who were callused towards those who were suffering around them. But when one looks closely at the first four beatitudes in Matthew's account (vv. 3, 4, 5, and 6), they will also see a progression of stages in which one moves through. One could say it is a process in which one dies unto themselves. And once this process is completed, the child of God will then emerge from it possessing a merciful spirit instead of a merciful attitude (v. 7).

³ Blessed are the poor in spirit, for theirs is the kingdom of heaven.
⁴ Blessed are those who mourn, for they shall be comforted.
⁵ Blessed are the meek, for they shall inherit the earth.
⁶ Blessed are those who hunger and thirst for righteousness, for they shall be satisfied.

⁷ Blessed are the merciful, for they shall receive mercy.

What is the difference between a merciful spirit and a merciful attitude? Although an attitude can involve the heart, it is more of a mental state whereas a spirit represents the complete *melding* together of the heart and mind and thus creating within one a hardened near unbreakable concrete trait. Though their personality, which makes them distinct, stays the same, their character will be as that of all of God's children, for they too will walk in love and truth towards all. So, the difference is that one's attitude can change quickly and easily while the spirit of a person does not.

Now one will not only emerge from this process with a merciful spirit, but they will also emerge with a heart that is pure. This is not to say that one will no longer sin (1 John 1:8), but it is to say that sin will have lost its appeal. In other words, the spirit of sin within them will have become neutralized by the Holy Spirit. It will no longer have the controlling influence over them as it once did. Then, as a result of these changes, the child of God will then be able to truly walk as a peacemaker.

I would like to now point out that in Jesus' list of beatitudes the merciful (v.7) came before the pure in heart (v.8). However, in his sermon Jesus began with the pure in heart in 5:21-37 and then addressed the merciful in 6:14-15 and 7:1-2. Why is this? This change is because the process is as follows, which is what this book has been following all along:

The Old Self	Pure in heart–One will seek to remove the sins of one's heart. (5:21-37)	But will see how frequently they sin
	Merciful–One will seek to walk in a forgiving/nonjudgmental way. (6:14-15 & 7:1-2)	But will fail due to their pride.
	Peacemaker–One will seek to walk according to Jesus' teachings. (5:38-48)	But will struggle with a love for world/self
Death	One will come to see their true level of sinfulness and become broken by it. (5:3-6) They will then call upon God for help and will receive the Holy Spirit into their heart. (Matthew 7:7-11 & Luke 11:13)	
A New Creation	Merciful–Impacted by God's mercy, they will now possess a merciful spirit instead of attitude. (5:7)	For their pride is now shattered and removed
	Pure in heart–Although they will still stumble, sin has lost its appeal. (5:8)	For they are now free from the power of sin
	Peacemaker–The world will no longer have a hold on them, and they can now walk in love towards all. (5:9)	For God is now their dominant love

To get a better understanding of this process, in which one dies unto themselves, lets now turn to the first of the initial four beatitudes found in Matthew 5:3. In this verse Jesus says **Blessed are the poor in spirit, for theirs is the kingdom of heaven.** The word "blessed" is simply a way of saying one has become fortunate in that the favor of God has fallen upon them. With this in mind, the poor in spirit are indeed fortunate for God has chosen them. He has sent forth his Spirit to enlighten them to their true sinful state. But this realization of who they really are can come at different times and in different ways. In other words, it is not the same for everyone. For instance, there are some, who upon hearing the gospel for the first time, will instantly receive clarity from the Holy Spirit. They will see the full extent of their sinfulness. But then there are some who will hear the gospel many times, and then suddenly they will be given clarity by the Spirit. And then there are some, like me, who will partially experience this, and as a result, they will receive the gospel and trust in the Lord Jesus Christ for their salvation, but they will not have a changed life. But at the appointed moment in time, the Holy Spirit will then fully enlighten them to their true sinful state. Thus, for us this becomes a gradual process.

Now why is this? In my case, the Holy Spirit was simply needing time to teach and to lead me to true repentance, and once I learned what true repentance was and began to try to walk in love, it was then when I discovered my true sinful state. And let us not forget denial, for I often struggled with accepting the fact that something was wrong. For a while, I simply refused to accept what the Holy Spirit was telling me, but in time I did, as you will, for the Holy Spirit does not fail.

But regardless of when or how this happens, the result is the same, every child of God will at some point in time come to see themselves for who they really are. But Jesus assured those who experienced this that the kingdom of heaven was theirs. His statement thus reflects assurance in that what God has begun in one's life he will see it through.

One will then read in verse 4, **Blessed are those who mourn...** Those who become aware of their sinful condition will start to grieve. They will do this for they will come to realize they cannot change on their own. They are helplessly stuck in their sinful state. And the reason why they grieve and mourn is because they have come to possess a "love for God" within their heart, which by the way is another inner working of the Holy Spirit (John 5:42 & Romans 5:5). Now it is this love for God which is the key for it is what makes the difference between the weeds and the wheat. It is what drives the child of God to want to be like God. It is what motivates them to keep trying to walk in love even when they continue to fail. And the reason why they continue to fail is because the spirit of sin within them still has power over them. And even though they may fight it and fight it, they still will not be able to break the hold it has on them. So, they are tormented, and they mourn. But Jesus assured them **they shall be comforted**. But keep in mind that this is not about salvation, it is about the Holy Spirit leading the child of God to genuine repentance.

Now the child of God will not stay in this state forever, for what will happen is that they will reach a point in which they will become spiritually broken. They will become as the tax collector who beat his chest and cried out to the heavenly Father to be merciful to him, for he was a sinner (Luke 18:9-14). And once again this can all take place suddenly or over a period of time.

But what this state of brokenness produces is then seen in verse 5 when Jesus says, **Blessed are the meek, for they shall inherit the earth.** Though meekness can be viewed as one who is weak or timid, the biblical meaning of the word is different, for it was used to describe the Son of God (2 Corinthians 10:1). But Jesus was not weak or timid for a glimpse of his power can be seen in Matthew 26:52, **Then Jesus said to him, "Put your sword back into its place. For all who live by the sword will perish by the sword.** ^{53} **Do you think that I cannot appeal to my Father, and he will at once send me more than twelve legions of angels?** Since Jesus did not destroy his enemies but chose instead to submit to the way of love and to the Father's plan, the biblical word for "meekness" should then be viewed in this way. It is one who submits to the Way of love and to the will of God. Thus, one is gentle, patient, kind, and nonaggressive towards those who show aggression towards them. Yet, at the same time, one will be bold and fearless when it comes to sharing the gospel and standing for truth and righteousness. And they will also be unmovable when it comes to anyone placing pressure on them into doing something which is contrary to the will of God.

Yet, this meekness cannot be achieved unless one first becomes humbled. In Matthew 11:29 one will read were Jesus called out to his followers and said, **Take my yoke upon you, and learn from me, for I am gentle and lowly of heart**... Jesus urged his followers to study him in order to be like him. They are to take his yoke of being gentle towards others and lowly of heart upon themselves (Philippians 2:1-9). Humility then is simply the absence of pride. But what is wrong with pride? When it comes to walking in love, pride causes one to focus on oneself whereas love is about focusing on others. Thus, the two will conflict. One will read in 1 Peter 5:5, **...Clothe yourselves, all of you, with humility toward one another, for "God opposes the proud but gives grace to the humble."** So, with this in mind, though Jesus was never with the sin of pride (Philippians 2:5-8), and since God opposes the proud, one's pride must therefore be removed, *and this is what the first two steps accomplish.* And once pride has been removed and one has become humbled and is in a spirit of meekness, one will then be able to call upon God their Father for help. This again is seen in the parable of the Pharisee and the Tax Collector:

⁹ He also told this parable to some who trusted in themselves that they were righteous, and treated others with contempt: ¹⁰ "Two men went up into the temple to pray, one a Pharisee and the other a tax collector. ¹¹ The Pharisee, standing by himself, prayed thus: 'God, I thank you that I am not like other men, extortioners, unjust, adulterers, or even like this tax collector. ¹² I fast twice a week; I give tithes of all that I get.' ¹³ But the tax collector, standing far off, would not even lift up his eyes to heaven, but beat his breast, saying, 'God, be merciful to me, a sinner!' ¹⁴ I tell you, this man went down to his house justified, rather than the other. For everyone who exalts himself will be humbled, but the one who humbles himself will be exalted." (Luke 18:9-14)

Notice how God rejected the self-righteous Pharisee. Since the Pharisee was blinded to the sin within his heart, he then became prideful, which then caused him to treat others with contempt. It was for this reason then that God opposed him. However, God had mercy on the humbled and broken tax collector who called out to him for help. Pride is therefore a sin of the heart which must be extinguished, and thus is the reason why Jesus said it would only be the meek who will inherit the future new earth.

Then the last of the first four beatitudes, which represents the final phase of the dying process, is found in verse 6, **Blessed are those who hunger and thirst for righteousness,**

for they shall be satisfied. With the removal of one's pride, the child of God will come forth from this event with a spirit of meekness, which will then allow them to purify their hearts and to walk in love. However, although they may have had a changed life, in that they have become free from the power of the spirit of sin within them, they will still have sin in their life (1 John 1:8). So, with this in mind, this final phase represents what the child of God will have to endure until their time on earth is complete. Because of their love for God and their desire to please him and to be like him, they will strive to be holy as he is holy. But no matter how hard they try; they will never be able to perfectly walk in love (Matthew 5:48). Thus, they will hunger and thirst for the righteousness of God in which they cannot achieve. The Apostle Paul wrote in Philippians 3:12-14:

¹² Not that I have already obtained this or am already perfect, but I press on to make it my own, because Christ Jesus has made me his own. ¹³ Brothers, I do not consider that I have made it my own. But one thing I do: forgetting what lies behind and straining forward to what lies ahead, ¹⁴ I press on toward the goal for the prize of the upward call of God in Christ Jesus.

But nonetheless, they will have nothing to fear, for although they will never be able to obtain God's level of perfect righteousness, Jesus did. Therefore, he reassures the children of God when he says, **for they shall be satisfied.**

It is now time for me to ask this question, "Have you ever been humbled and broken by the Holy Spirit?" This would definitely be something in which you would remember. But this event must happen in your life in order for you to change. Your old self must die on the cross with Jesus in order for you to become free from your sinful addictions and to walk in newness of life. Now I am speaking from experience for this has happened in my life, and I know it can happen in yours. So, if this has not yet taken place in your life, then there is something you can do.

For Existing Baptized Believers

For those who have already believed and accepted the true gospel of Jesus Christ and have also been baptized, if you experienced spiritual brokenness at the time you believed, then the question is this; "Was it a life changing event?" In other words, did it result with you coming out of the event with a spirit of meekness? I ask this question, for as we have learned, only those who have a spirit of meekness can truly walk in love. If you did, then this book has simply been an affirmation of your experience and an encouragement for you to continue to walk in love and truth. However, if not, then you are like me, in that you felt conviction of sin and maybe some spiritual brokenness, but not a life changing event. If this is the case, then the first step is for you to repent. But please bear in mind that as you seek to walk in love and truth, you will soon discover something about yourself. You will discover if you are a weed or wheat. If you are a weed, then you will be unable to tolerate the Way. However, if you do belong to God, then you will begin to see the complete and amazing value of love and your appreciation of it will grow, for this is also the work of the Holy Spirit within you. This is not to say that the Way will not be difficult to follow, for it will be, but it is to say that *you will not be able to abandon the path*. And it is once again because you have a love of God within you, which is from the Holy Spirit.

THE PREREQUISITE TO CHANGE

Now on the subject of seeing the evidence of the Holy Spirit in one's life, when one looks at scripture one will at times read of people who began to speak in tongues. When they did, this was a clear indication that the person had received the Holy Spirit. But since this did not take place in every instance (Acts 8:26-40; 16:11-15; & 25-34), one can conclude that it was not the primary sign. So, what was? It was when one began to genuinely walk in both love and truth (1 Corinthians 13:1). Love and truth are therefore the primary signs of the Spirit's presence in one's life and not the gift of speaking in tongues.

Returning again to spiritual brokenness, if you are indeed a child of God, then as time goes by you will begin to see your true sinful state. You will not only start to see your present sins more clearly, but you will also begin to recall the sins of your past. Once again, this is the work of the Holy Spirit convicting you.

But what do I mean by seeing your true sinful sate? The best way to describe this process is by sharing with you a story from when I served in the U.S. Marine Corp Infantry. In the infantry, there would be times when we would spend weeks out in the field. Now going that length of time without bathing, we knew we were dirty, but yet we could not fully fathom the extent of our filthiness. But when we got back to the barracks, got all cleaned up, and then went to get our cloths to wash them, it was then, at that moment, when we fully realized just how filthy we really were, for the stench of our clothes would nearly knock us down! Well, this same thing will happen to you, but in this case, you will come to realize the true level of your sinfulness. Right now, even though you know, you don't know, but you will.

So, as the Holy Spirit continues to reveal to you the depth of your sinfulness, you will begin to reach a point in which the weight of regret from your past and present sins will become so unbearable that the pride within you will begin to shatter. When this happens, the second step is to not close the door to these feelings but to let the flood of guilt, shame, and remorse sweep over you. Allow yourself to become broken before the Lord your God.

Then the third step, as previous illustrated with the parable of the Pharisee and the Tax Collector, can be seen in Jesus' Sermon on the Mount, which in Matthew 7:7-11 one will read:

7 "Ask, and it will be given to you; seek, and you will find; knock, and it will be opened to you. 8 For everyone who asks receives, and the one who seeks finds, and to the one who knocks it will be opened. 9 Or which one of you, if his son asks him for bread, will give him a stone? 10 Or if he asks for a fish, will give him a serpent? 11 If you then, who are evil, know how to give good gifts to your children, how much more will your Father who is in heaven give good things to those who ask him!"

At first glance Jesus seems to be simply encouraging people to pray, and in a way, he is, but not as one might think. One should keep in mind that throughout his sermon, Jesus has been speaking to those who could hear (Matthew 11:15; 13:9, 43; & 15:10), which is to say, those who had been given the ability by the Holy Spirit to understand what Jesus was saying. So, in effect, Jesus had been teaching and encouraging these chosen individuals to live the way of God. But as shown, though they would seek to do this, they would fail and eventually become spiritually broken. So, in this passage Jesus was revealing to them just what they needed to do when this event took place, which is for them to then call upon God for help, and the reason they could do this was because *they were already his children* (Please refer back to v.11).

But how would their heavenly Father help them? Jesus said he would provide them with good things. Since in Matthew's passage it is unclear as to what exactly Jesus was referring to, one must look to Luke's parallel passage in 11:13 for the answer, **If you then, who are evil, know how to give good gifts to your children, how much more will the heavenly Father give the Holy Spirit to those who ask him!** So, the gift in which Jesus was speaking of was the gift of the Holy Spirit. Now once again, since they were already considered to be children of God, the Holy Spirit had already been with them leading them to this point. Jesus was therefore telling them that when they became spiritually broken, by their inability to follow his Way, then all they needed to do was call upon God their Father for help. God would then help them by allowing his Spirit to move from being *with* them to being *in* them. And because the Holy Spirit moved to being in them, they would then be able to walk as he walked (1 John 2:6).

With this being said, because of your present belief in the true gospel of Jesus Christ and of your desire to repent, God's Spirit has already been with you this whole time. He has opened your mind enabling you to understand the gospel and to comprehend the complete value of love. And because you have a love of God within you, you are therefore already his child. So, with this assurance, as you continue to strive to walk in love and truth, and when you reach a crisis of heart and mind, with a humble heart and a meek spirit, you can then call upon God your Father for help and he will answer your prayer. And when this moment comes, simply convey your love to the Father and how desperately you desire to walk as his Son, Jesus Christ. Convey to the Father how you cannot do this alone, and how you need him to help you by having his Spirit move from being *with* you to dwelling *in* your heart. Then, in faith, thank God for hearing your prayer and fulfilling the promise he has made to you in his word.

Then, begin walking in love and truth again. But now that your pride is gone and you now possess the spirit of meekness, you will come to see this has made all the difference in the world. You may not at first notice a change, but as the days go by, you will begin to notice that things seem different. You will notice that the things which used to tempt you will no longer have the same attraction as they once did. This is because you are no longer enslaved to sin! You have become a changed person, a new creation!

Now regarding baptism, there is no need for you to become rebaptized if you have believed in the true gospel of Jesus Christ, felt his presence in your life, and then later experienced spiritual brokenness. This delay was simply the result of you either not being taught what true repentance was, or you were in denial of your sinful state, or you were just unready to accept the Way. But whatever the case may be, you were saved the moment you believed in the true gospel of Jesus Christ, the Holy Spirit just had to work with you for a while in order to bring you to repentance. However, if you feel uncertain in that the Spirit of God has been with you, then by all means become rebaptized. Follow your conscience! There is absolutely nothing wrong with being rebaptized.

The Initial Prayer

Now it is imperative that you understand something: salvation does not come to one by a prayer, *for this is a work*!

Salvation comes to one the moment the Spirit opens one's eyes to understanding the gospel and they believe it with an accepting heart. This was why Paul wrote in Romans 10:10, **For with the heart one believes and is justified, and with the mouth one confesses and is saved.** Because of this, one will never see in scripture one praying to God and then receiving the Holy Spirit (See Acts 2:37-38; 10:44-48; and 16:30-33). Now there were times when the apostles prayed, while laying hands on individuals, and they then received the Spirit, yet this did not take place throughout the New Testament (Acts 2:38-39; 8:26-40; 10:34-48; 16:25-40; & 18:8-9). So, one can conclude that the laying on of hands of the apostles were simply key moments in the growth of the Church in which God wanted certain individuals to know that salvation was through Jesus Christ, and that they needed to adhere to the apostle's teachings.

Now it is my belief that the practice of praying for the Holy Spirit to come into one's life, upon one's initial belief in the gospel, has come about as the result of some people experiencing spiritual brokenness at the moment when they first believed. But what this has done is that it has confused "spiritual brokenness" with one's "belief in the gospel" as being when one actually receives the Holy Spirit. Not only is this unbiblical, as has been shown in this book, but what this does is that it confuses those who then experience spiritual brokenness later in their walk with the Lord. And because of this practice, these individuals will then think that they had just become saved, when in actuality, they had been saved at the moment when they first believed in the gospel. But this is not the worst part, for what this practice also does is that it allows individuals, referring to the weeds, to reject true repentance of walking in love and truth, and to trust fully in the prayer that they made back when they first believed in the gospel. Since they prayed a prayer, asking God to send his Spirit into their life, they will claim to have received the Holy Spirit at this time, and thus they are saved, even though there is no evidence which reveals the Spirit's presence in their life.

With this being said, I have come to believe that the initial prayer in which one should pray upon their belief in the gospel should be a prayer of thankfulness, acknowledgment, acceptance, and commitment. It is not a time for one to ask for the Holy Spirit to come into their life for he is already with the believer. So, upon one's belief in the gospel, one should pray to God their Father thanking him for sending them the gift of salvation, his Holy Spirit, who has opened their eyes so they could understand the gospel. Then, they should humbly acknowledge to God their Father how they are a sinner unworthy of such a gift, but they wholeheartedly accept the gospel of Jesus Christ his Son as the truth, and because of this, they fully commit to following their Way. And then they should humbly appeal to their heavenly Father to move his Spirit from being *with* them to being *in* them, for they cannot walk in love and truth without him. And then, they should close their prayer by once again thanking God for saving them, and then begin walking in faith.

For New Unbaptized Believers

Now if you are one who has just recently begun to believe in the gospel of Jesus Christ, then you should immediately begin by praying the initial prayer (as stated above) and repenting. With this being said, repentance not only begins with you walking in love and truth, but it also begins with you becoming baptized in Jesus' name (Acts 2:38-39). Not only did

Jesus command it, but when you are being baptized, you are publicly proclaiming to all that you are now one who believes and accepts the gospel of Jesus Christ, and that you have become committed to following his Way.

But please be aware of this fact, as previously stated, as you begin to walk in both love and truth, it is then when you will discover if you are a weed or wheat. If you cannot live Christ's way, then you are a weed. But keep in mind also that the Way will be difficult to travel. You will struggle. However, as previously stated, the greatest sign of God's presence in your life will be the fact that no matter how difficult the path becomes, you will never be able to let it go. You will never be able to give up trying to follow the way of God. This is due to you having a love of God within you and you have come to value his Way too much.

So, as you begin walking this difficult path of love and truth, if you have yet to experience spiritual brokenness, then you too will soon encounter this life changing event. This is because the Holy Spirit has been *with* you, opening your eyes to the truth of the gospel and to the complete and wonderful value of love, but he has yet to move from being *with* you to being *in* your heart.

Now when the Holy Spirit begins to enlighten you to the true extent of your sinful condition, embrace it. Do not resist but allow yourself to feel guilty and ashamed for what you have done. Let yourself become broken before the Lord. And when this moment comes, simply convey your love to the Father and how desperately you desire to walk as his Son, Jesus Christ. Convey to the heavenly Father how you cannot do this alone, and how you need him to help you by having his Spirit move from being *with* you to dwelling *in* your heart. Then, in faith, thank God your Father for hearing your prayer and fulfilling the promise he has made to you in his word, and begin walking in love and truth again. Then, within time you too will start to notice that a change has taken place in your life. You too will soon realize that you have become free from the power of sin. And once again, this is the power of the gospel!

Closing Remarks

Since we have now come to the end of the book, it is my hope and prayer that you will not only accept Christ's way but that you will also share this message among those within your church. It is my belief that this message will bring about new life into the churches of God, for when God's people fully embrace his commandments, which are to believe in him and to walk in love towards God and others, then amazing things will happen. The world will then begin to see the true power of the gospel of Jesus Christ, and people will be drawn to the light as they see the love of God within his people. As Jesus said to his disciples in John 13:34-35, **A new commandment I give to you, that you love one another: just as I have loved you, you also are to love one another. ³⁵ By this all people will know that you are my disciples, if you have love for one another.**

So, it is my hope and prayer that as this message begins to spread among the churches of God, it will be the spark that will ignite the last great revival within our country. A revival that will spread across our nation, like a wildfire, revealing the true gospel of Jesus Christ to our cities, our country, and to the world. Yet, we must hurry for I also believe the time of the great tribulation of man is upon us. Therefore, my brothers and sisters, play time is over, and it is now time for us to step up to the plate and become what God has called us to be. So, as I start my journey down the path of love, will you please join me in following the Way of our Lord and Savior Jesus Christ? Will you too become a Waytraveler?

I will now close this book with a final warning from the Son of God, the one in whom we all will one day stand before in judgement, for in Luke 12:42-48 one will read:

[42] **And the Lord said, "Who then is the faithful and wise manager, whom his master will set over his household, to give them their portion of food at the proper time?** [43] **Blessed is that servant whom his master will find so doing when he comes.** [44] **Truly, I say to you, he will set him over all his possessions.** [45] **But if that servant says to himself, 'My master is delayed in coming,' and begins to beat the male and female servants, and to eat and drink and get drunk,** [46] **the master of that servant will come on a day when he does not expect him and at an hour he does not know, and will cut him in pieces and put him with the unfaithful.** [47] **And that servant who knew his master's will but did not get ready or act according to his will, will receive a severe beating.** [48] **But the one who did not know, and did what deserved a beating, will receive a light beating. Everyone to whom much was given, of him much will be required, and from him to whom they entrusted much, they will demand the more."**

"He who has ears to hear, let him hear." – Matthew 11:15

Summary Questions

1. According to Paul, in order for one to change one must become _____ with Christ. Why?

2. The first four beatitudes in Matthew's account reflect a progression of stages in which one moves through.
   a. The poor in spirit are those who…

   b. Those who mourn are those who…

   c. The meek are those who emerge from the possess with a _____ spirit.
   d. Those who hunger and thirst are those who…

3. What is the difference between a merciful spirit and a merciful attitude?

4. How should the biblical word for "meekness" be viewed?

5. Meekness cannot be achieved unless one first becomes _____.

6. Why is it so important for one's pride to be removed?

7. The greatest sign that you are wheat instead of a weed is that no matter how difficult the path becomes, you will never be able to let it go simply because you _____ God.

Notes

THE WAYTRAVELERS

Made in the USA
Middletown, DE
07 October 2022